DO YOU KNOW . . .

- Loneliness, relationship problems, retirement, and even happy milestones such as graduating and buying a house can trigger depression.

- Depression is common after surgery, and one type of medication offers quick relief . . . but many doctors are unaware of it.

- Not all antidepressant medications have the same side effects; talk to your doctor to find the medication that is right for you.

- Depression runs in families and women are more vulnerable to the disease than men.

- Depression can manifest itself differently, depending on your cultural, religious, or ethnic background.

- Severely depressed people feel worse in the morning than at night. In lesser degrees of depression, the reverse is usually true.

FIND OUT MORE IN . . .

**IF YOU THINK YOU HAVE
DEPRESSION**

Look for these other Dell Guides for Mental Health

If You Think You Have Panic Disorder

If You Think You Have an Eating Disorder

If You Think You Have a Sleep Disorder

If You Think You Have Seasonal Affective Disorder

A DELL MENTAL HEALTH GUIDE

If You Think You Have

DEPRESSION

Roger Granet, M.D.,
and
Robin K. Levinson

A DELL BOOK

Published by
Dell Publishing
a division of
Bantam Doubleday Dell Publishing Group, Inc.
1540 Broadway
New York, New York 10036

ISBN: 0-440-22541-8

Printed in the United States of America

Published simultaneously in Canada

April 1998

10   9   8   7   6   5   4   3   2   1

OPM

Dedications

To the other four men on our "basketball team of
life"—Hank Alpert, Peter Ehrenberg, Larry Gelber,
and Jerry Wichtel. Your goodness and jump shots
sustain me. And to all my patients, with deep
respect.

—Roger Granet, M.D.

To Rabbi Paula Goldberg, for her friendship,
wisdom, advice, and scholarship

—Robin K. Levinson

Acknowledgments

Thanks to . . .

All the depression sufferers who have courageously shared their stories and suggestions that helped make this book possible;

Laurie Martin, Lesley Meisoll, and Clifford Taylor, M.D., for the generosity of their skill and encouragement;

Michael Robinson, M.D., and pyschiatric nurse Barbara Curran for their insights into electroshock therapy; and

Literary agent Judith Riven for her editing and matchmaking talents.

This book is written for educational purposes only and is not intended to replace the advice of a health professional. All treatment information is based on research findings current at the time the book was written. All names of depression patients and their family members have been changed, and some details were altered to further mask people's identities.

Contents

Foreword

*I cry during the day and into the night. I am weary
with my groaning. My heart is sore. My strength is
dried up. Lighten my eyes, or I may sleep the sleep
of death.*

These words powerfully capture the essence of depression. Were they written by a contemporary poet groping for meaning as we approach the next millennium? They very well could have been. But in fact these are the poignant words of King David, immortalized in the Psalms of the Old Testament, written some three thousand years ago. As King David's words suggest, depression is no newcomer to the human experience.

Depression is as devastating as it is timeless. It stalks its victims like a thief in the night, slowly robbing their self-worth, joy, and passion for life. It is a mental illness that knows no prejudice and spares no ethnic group, age, or gender. Because it is underrecognized and undertreated, depression causes millions to suffer unnecessarily. In King David's time, there was no sophisticated mental health knowledge. In our time, depression has become the most treatable of all the emotional disorders—so treatable that almost any sufferer can be helped.

Thanks to remarkable advances in diagnosis and treatment, those struggling with a depressive disorder—and their loved ones—have every reason to be hopeful. They also have the right to cutting-edge interventions, such as psychotherapies developed especially for depressed patients, a wide array of potent antidepressants, and various other modern treatment modalities.

As its title suggests, this book targets all who think they have depression. It also can be of enormous benefit to those who have been diagnosed with any of the depressive disorders. This book aims to educate readers about their illness and guide them toward a positive future filled with hope and psychological peace.

The audience for this book is, regrettably, wide. Each year, approximately 18 million Americans are struck with clinical depression, yet only a fraction are appropriately and adequately treated. The annual cost to our economy, including work loss and health costs, is almost $50 billion. Only advanced coronary artery disease results in more disability days; only arthritis causes more chronic pain.

The very word *depression* is frequently tossed about with little thought of its clinical definition, much less its social ramifications. One major advance is the development of rigorous, valid, and reliable criteria to define depression. In easy-to-follow terms, these criteria are spelled out in the pages that follow. As readers will see, depression takes many forms and wears many masks. Major depression, the most common manifestation, is characterized by sadness, crying spells, lack of interest, and difficulty experiencing pleasure, along with changes in sleep, appetite, energy, and concentration. In addition, one's sense of self-worth is whittled away, often replaced by inappropriate feelings of guilt.

Of course, the most dangerous consequence of this painful experience is the potential for suicide, an understandable but unnecessary outcome. As recently

as twenty-five years ago, almost nothing could be
done to prevent someone from committing suicide.
Today, these tragedies can often be averted because
depression has become eminently treatable.

What makes mental health professionals so confi-
dent in their abilities to help depressed people overcome their illness? Psychiatrists, psychologists, and
social workers are beneficiaries of an explosion in research, technological advances, and clinical experience that have been accumulating over the past three
decades. Sophisticated investigations into the psychological, biological, and sociological causes and
treatments of this malignant, emotional disease have
yielded wonderful results.

Psychological studies have provided important
new data concerning the emotional causes of depression. Building upon early Freudian concepts of
loss, guilt, and anger turned against the self, researchers and theorists have expanded our insight
into the many internal psychological events that may
lead to depression. Additionally, there has been re-
warding work into how abnormal psychology can
affect a person's thinking and relationships. These
findings have led to the evolution of psychotherapies
especially suited for depression. Unlike the costly,
time-consuming, traditional Freudian psychoanalysis, modern therapeutic techniques are briefer and
more focused. One of the new modalities—brief dynamic psychotherapy—uses Freudian concepts, but
more specifically targets the understanding of past
and present feelings as they relate to a current
depressive episode. Cognitive therapy was developed
to help depressed individuals focus on their distorted thought patterns and learn how to break
those patterns. Finally, interpersonal psychotherapy,
the newest psychotherapeutic modality, places an

emphasis on understanding how unhealthy relationships may lead to depression.

Used alone or in combination with medication, all
three of these relatively new "talking treatments"
have consistently been shown to both alleviate depression and offer a protective effect from future
episodes.

Perhaps the largest body of research to improve
treatment outcomes centers on the biology of depression. Technological advances permit researchers to
use new brain-imaging methods, such as positron
emission tomography (PET scans), to observe how
the brain functions during depression. This and other
imaging and laboratory techniques reveal exciting
clues for pinpointing the physiological causes of this
terrible mood disorder. Other areas of research have
focused on neurotransmitters, the chemical messengers of the brain that become altered in depression.

In addition, genetic research has begun to isolate
abnormalities on chromosomes in those who are depressed. These discoveries could lead to gene therapy
in the not-too-distant future. Another prong of genetic investigation looks at family trees. By deepening
our understanding of how depression is inherited, it
may soon be possible to predict scientifically who is
predisposed. In a sense, that is already possible. If one
or more of your parents or siblings ever suffered from
depression, you should consider yourself at risk.

A most exciting by-product of biological research
has been the development of safer and more effective
antidepressant drugs. These medications work more
efficiently and have fewer side effects than the earlier
medications developed in the late 1960s. Doctors
have at their disposal numerous antidepressants,
which may be thoughtfully and carefully integrated
into the total treatment of the depressed patient.

Choosing drugs and dosages is expected to become much easier; scientists are now developing a series of blood tests that should tell us which antidepressant would be most effective for a given individual.

Even the controversial treatment electroconvulsive therapy (also known as ECT or "shock treatments") has undergone dramatic changes in recent years. Modern techniques reduce physical risk factors while lessening the potential for memory loss.

Yet another reason for optimism in dealing with depression focuses on sociological variables. A number of sophisticated studies have examined the external factors that can spawn, intensify, or prolong a depressive episode. In particular, data have led researchers to focus on loss. Examples of loss include the death of a loved one, divorce, or becoming unemployed. Through bettering our understanding of loss and other environmental stressors, we have become far more effective in creating appropriate treatment plans.

Conversely, research has also identified factors that may actually lighten the burden of depression. For example, exercise and music, as well as meditation and other Eastern relaxation techniques, can sometimes help people recover from, and perhaps prevent, mild to moderate depressive symptoms.

A final area of research concerns itself with the positive and negative impact of family and friends. Sociologists and social psychiatrists have identified a number of steps that loved ones can take to help patients deal with their depressed moods. In addition, research into the "family dynamic"—the interaction among family members—has yielded new, more effective approaches in family therapy.

With all this research serving as a backdrop, the stigma that has surrounded depression and other mental illnesses for centuries is beginning to loosen its grip. In part, this is due to the fine work of self-help organizations, such as the National Depressive and Manic-Depressive Association, which provides education and understanding for those with depression. Toward the same end, the American Psychiatric Association has created National Depression Awareness Week in October to shed more light on depression and to encourage clinically depressed people to obtain treatment. Persuading health insurers to pay for those treatments is getting easier now, thanks to new laws and policies requiring mental health coverage to be as comprehensive as medical coverage.

Beyond the scientific and political aspects of depression are the human beings—the mental health professionals and the depressed people—who have the power to create a therapeutic environment. Mental health professionals, for the most part, are bright, well-trained, committed, and compassionate. The depressed people who seek them out have found the courage and conviction to face their disorder head-on and to make the most of what science has to offer them. And in the vast majority of these cases, they are putting to rest their inner turmoil and reclaiming their lives.

In biblical times, King David had nothing but faith to overcome depression. Had he lived today, he could rely on his faith—plus the wisdom of modern science and humanity.

—**Roger Granet, M.D., F.A.P.A.**
Clinical Associate Professor of Psychiatry
Cornell University Medical College

Morristown, New Jersey, 1997

Chapter One

DEPRESSION: DEFINITIONS AND OVERVIEW

Depression is one of the most common and misunderstood mental health problems of our time. Each year, almost 18 million Americans become depressed. Depression alters not only your mood; its deleterious effects resonate through your thoughts, body, and behaviors. Depression can be a one-time event, an episodic problem, or a chronic illness lasting years. In bipolar disorder, episodes of dreadful "lows" alternate with inappropriate euphoric moods. Yet, even though depression is a potentially life-threatening illness, there is good news for anyone suffering from this disorder: it is highly treatable, and nearly everyone who gets appropriate help can recover— and learn how to minimize or prevent any future episodes.

Depression is believed to have been around for at least 2,500 years, and descriptions of the experience are myriad. Some of the more familiar are "a stormy cloud," "a downward spiral," "a bottomless pit," "looking at the world through gauze," "lost in a fog," "a huge weight on my shoulders," "moving in slow motion," "down in the dumps," "walking through mud," "feeling empty inside," and "trapped in sadness." Perhaps some of these descriptions reflect how

you have felt or are feeling right now. If you or someone close to you has experienced feelings of depression, you need not feel hopeless. By opening this
book, you have taken the first step on the road back
to mental health. The following pages will answer
many of the questions you may have about depression
and will provide the latest information on the various
treatment options. This book can also help you decide
whether you need treatment at all, for not everyone
who feels "down in the dumps" has a true mental
health problem.

What is depression?

Everyone feels blue now and then; sadness is a normal, healthy, human emotion. Most of the time, sadness, emptiness, and related feelings are short-lived,
lasting only a few hours or days. If, however, your
spirits remain low for two or more consecutive weeks
and hamper your ability to work, tend to your family,
get along with people, or otherwise derive pleasure
from life, you may be suffering an abnormal mood
disturbance, or what doctors term "depression,"
"major depression," "unipolar depression," "clinical
depression," "affective disorder," or "depressive illness." It may help to know that depression is so pervasive that it is sometimes called the "common cold"
of psychiatric illnesses.

Many well-known and highly successful people
are believed to have suffered from depression, including Anne Sexton, Vincent Van Gogh, Robert E. Lee,
Winston Churchill, Diane Arbus, Sylvia Plath, John
Keats, Mozart, and Beethoven. On April 11, 1997,
prizewinning author Michael Dorris committed suicide at age fifty-two. His estranged wife, Louise Er-

drich, told *The New York Times* that Dorris had been severely depressed for many years.

Cases like Dorris's fall on the farthest end of a continuum of depressive illness, which range from mild to life-threatening. Symptoms of a major depressive disorder include feelings of hopelessness, helplessness, worthlessness, guilt, pessimism, and sadness. These feelings persist throughout most of the day, nearly every day. Other signs may be fatigue, irritability, trouble concentrating, and a variety of physical ailments—abdominal pain, palpitations, headaches, and digestive disorders, to name a few—that do not respond to medical treatment. Clinically depressed individuals often lose interest in work or other activities, including sex. Eating patterns may change, leading to significant weight loss or gain. Some feel restless or profoundly bored. Loss of energy and disrupted sleep patterns are also quite common. If you are depressed, you may try to avoid family gatherings and social situations. In the severest of cases, sufferers become preoccupied with death. They entertain thoughts of suicide or engage in life-threatening behaviors. Fifteen percent of severely depressed people wind up killing themselves; the suicide rate among people with major depression is thirty times that of the general population. Wherever the term "depression" appears in this book, it always refers to the abnormal, diagnosable mood disturbance—not normal sadness, which dissipates within a few hours or days and does not warrant professional attention.

Although any age group is vulnerable, even young children, the average age of onset of depression is the late twenties to late thirties. For a variety of complex reasons, women are more vulnerable than men to depression. According to researchers, as many as 26 percent of women and up to 12 percent of men will experience major depression at some point during their lives. Each year, about four out of every one hundred teenagers get clinically depressed. Nearly one third of depressed people also engage in some form of substance abuse or are dependent on alcohol or drugs, according to the National Institute of Mental Health (NIMH). Research has revealed another disturbing trend: The rate of depression is increasing among people born after 1945. Experts speculate that this may be related to single parenting, changing roles, and the everyday stresses of the postindustrial age.

Untreated, a major depressive episode usually lasts a minimum of six months. Dysthymia—a chronic, low-grade depression—lasts two years or more. People with depression cannot "snap out" of their low moods any more than diabetics can "snap out" of their need for insulin.

What are some of the triggers of depression?

For Cynthia, a thirty-one-year-old freelance writer, becoming a new mother to a premature baby triggered a severe depressive episode in 1993. The symptoms came on slowly, evolving from irritability and frequent crying spells to hopelessness, despair, and rage. Cynthia's postpartum depression (PPD) almost wrecked her marriage. "Like any depression, the PPD made open communication between us impossible," she says. "We got caught in a terrible cycle of me blaming my husband, Paul, for everything that went wrong, Paul getting angry, me getting more upset about his anger and blaming him for making me upset." By the time her daughter was five months old, Cynthia had grown so agitated and depressed that she couldn't eat or sleep. Only then did she consult a psychiatrist.

The first antidepressant Cynthia took didn't work, but the second one helped right away, possibly owing to a placebo effect. "Definitely within two to three weeks, though, the second antidepressant was making a real difference," she remembers. "This, in turn, helped me sort out which issues to deal with in therapy." Cynthia emphasizes that her journey back to mental health wasn't smooth. She had several relapses, exacerbated by premenstrual syndrome, before her depression lifted.

To her dismay, Cynthia's depressive symptoms returned during and after her second pregnancy, in 1996. "I did get very bad, but the medication helped so that the symptoms weren't prolonged," she says. "Also, being an experienced mother really helped."

Postpartum depression is one of several subcategories of clinical depression listed in the *Diagnostic and Statistical Manual of Mental Disorders—Fourth Edition*, or *DSM-IV* (American Psychiatric Association, 1994), the "bible" of mental illness. PPD probably results in part from major hormonal shifts associated with pregnancy and childbirth combined with the sudden, enormous responsibilities of caring for an infant. Other depression diagnoses listed in *DSM-IV* include:

• *Dysthymia* (diss-THY-mee-ah), a mild, chronic depression or despondency that lasts at least two years in adults and one year in children and adolescents. Dysthymia is sometimes referred to as "depressive personality" or "depressive temperament." If chronic depression is punctuated with episodes of severe depression, the disorder is known as "double depression." Up to 25 percent of people diagnosed with dysthymia will also suffer at least one major depressive episode.

• *Bipolar Disorder,* in which patients experience episodes of clinical depression and periods of mania—an elevated, expansive, or irritable mood—each of which lasts more than a week. During the manic stage, thoughts race through the patient's head, and he or she may talk incessantly. Grandiosity, reduced sleep, distractibility, and poor judgment are the other hallmarks of the manic phase of bipolar disorder. Bipolar disorder is also known as manic-depressive illness and manic depression.

• *Mixed Disorder,* in which there is evidence of depression and mania at the same time.

• *Atypical Depression.* Unlike people with typical depressions who can find no joy in life, people with atypical depression *can* enjoy pleasurable situations, although they are unable to seek out these situations. There are other differences, as well. Instead of having a decreased appetite and insomnia, these people generally eat and sleep more than usual. There are also reports of "leaden paralysis," or feelings of heaviness in the arms and legs. Atypically depressed people tend to be ultrasensitive to interpersonal rejection. Some authorities believe atypical depression may actually be more widespread than typical depression.

• *Cyclothymic (SI-clo-THI-mic) Disorder* is diagnosed when a person experiences repeated episodes of mild depression and mild mania over the course of at least two years (at least one year in children and adolescents).

• *Mood Disorder Due to a Medical Condition.* Depression can be symptomatic of several illnesses, most notably hypothyroidism. This form of depression goes away when the patient begins taking thyroid medication. Chapter Two will list other medical conditions known to cause depression.

• *Substance-Induced Mood Disorder,* which is caused by alcohol or prescription or illicit drugs. Hundreds, if not thousands, of legal medications list depression as a possible side effect. Alcohol itself is a depressant. In Chapter Three, you will find out which medications are most notorious for producing depression. You will also learn what you can do if you need one of those drugs to treat a chronic medical condition, such as high blood pressure.

• *Seasonal Affective Disorder* (SAD), also known as wintertime depression. In most cases, SAD victims become lethargic, sad, irritable, and unproductive beginning in October or November. Throughout the winter, they tend to oversleep and experience intense carbohydrate cravings, which lead to weight gain. When springtime comes, their depressed mood lifts, and their sleep and eating habits return to normal.* Another book in this series, *If You Think You Have Seasonal Affective Disorder,* is devoted to causes, symptoms, and treatments of SAD.

In extreme cases, depressive symptoms may include psychotic, catatonic, or melancholic features. Psychotic depressives suffer delusions or hallucinations, whose content may or may not be consistent with typical depressive themes of personal inadequacy, guilt, disease, death, nihilism, or deserved punishment. Catatonic depressives refuse, involuntarily, to move or be moved. Some uncontrollably repeat every word that's spoken to them. Melancholic

*Reprinted with permission from the *Diagnostic and Statistical Manual of Mental Disorders,* Fourth Edition. Copyright 1994 American Psychiatric Association.

features include the inability to feel much better, even temporarily, when something good happens. Depression can also be accompanied by significant anorexia or weight loss, or excessive or inappropriate guilt.

Why do people get depressed?

Depression is a complex phenomenon, and no one knows exactly why some people get depressed and others don't. Most researchers and clinicians would agree, however, that biology, psychology, and environment all factor into the equation, to varying degrees. If your depression is predominantly biological (physiological) in nature, symptoms generally occur for no apparent reason. If your personality type leaves you vulnerable to mood disorders, a negative life event—such as breaking up with a boyfriend or being demoted at work—can trigger a major depressive episode.

In Chapter Two, you will learn how to recognize symptoms of uncomplicated major depression, atypical depression, dysthymia, bipolar disorder, PPD, and other depression diagnoses. Chapter Three will discuss depression's major triggers and risk factors and include information on brain chemical abnormalities that appear to play an important role in who gets depressed and how severely. Certain depression-prone personality traits, such as low self-esteem and dependency, will be explored. This chapter will also tell you how mental health practitioners diagnose depression. In Chapter Four, you will find tips on navigating the mental health maze to find a qualified professional to help you. Cost of treatment and insurance issues also will be discussed.

Chapters Five through Seven take in-depth looks at the various treatments for depression, ranging from psychotherapy and antidepressants to electro-convulsive therapy, hospitalization, and self-help strategies, such as exercise and meditation. The pros and cons of alternative treatments, including the herb, St. John's wort, and acupuncture, also will be discussed.

Despite the many ways of alleviating depression, almost two out of three depressed people do not seek treatment, and half of those don't even realize they are clinically depressed. Emily suffered with major depression for months before seeing a psychiatrist. Getting treated, she says, "was like walking up from the subway into the light." Emily was one of the lucky ones because she obtained proper treatment. Historically, as few as one in ten depressed people who got professional help received adequate treatment, according to a nationwide community survey of psychiatric illnesses conducted around 1980. That dismal statistic has probably improved in recent years thanks to publicity campaigns sponsored by professional and patient groups.

The stigma that dissuades many depressed individuals from getting treatment is being addressed at the national level. In 1997, the Equal Employment Opportunity Commission announced rules designed to protect qualified workers from job discrimination if they have psychiatric or emotional problems. Furthermore, the EEOC said, employers may not ask job applicants if they have a history of mental problems. Celebrities, meanwhile, are beginning to speak publicly about their own battles with mental illness. One is journalist Mike Wallace of 60 Minutes fame, who has been hospitalized for depression. Having testified about his problem before Congress, Wallace told Newsweek he expects he'll be taking the antidepressant Zoloft every day for the rest of his life.

"And I'm quite content to do it," the 1996 article quoted him as saying.

Depression costs billions.

Obtaining prompt and proper treatment for your depression is vitally important, not only for you and your loved ones, but for society as a whole. When you combine health care expenses, worker absenteeism, decreased productivity, and premature death, the estimated cost of major depression, dysthymia, and bipolar disorder to our nation is about $43 billion annually, according to a study prepared for "The National Depressive and Manic-Depressive Association Consensus Statement on the Undertreatment of Depression" in 1996.

"Depression can be as debilitating as diabetes, arthritis, gastrointestinal disorders, back problems, or hypertension, in terms of physical and social functioning," says the consensus report, which appeared in the esteemed *Journal of the American Medical Association* in January 1997.

The cost of depression to our society can be reduced substantially through prevention, which is the topic of Chapter Eight. More than half of people who have recovered from one depressive episode will experience a recurrence. Fortunately, recurrent symptoms may be minimized or even prevented through the judicious use of antidepressants and other techniques. Suicide-prevention strategies also will be covered in Chapter Eight.

Because it can take several weeks before the benefits of your treatment kick in, knowing how to cope with depression on a day-to-day basis is extremely valuable. Chapter Nine suggests dozens of coping strategies you can try. Among them are immersing yourself in music, keeping a journal, avoiding isolation, and allowing yourself to feel awful in the morning. Additionally, this final chapter will suggest ways to help your loved ones help you.

Self-help groups for people with depression or manic depression abound in the United States; many of these groups are listed in the Resources section at the end of this book. A bibliography of other depression books will help you pursue this topic further.

In the meantime, know that as miserable as you may feel at this moment, the gray cloud hovering over you is not a permanent fixture in your life. The sooner you educate yourself about depression and seek out treatment, the faster you will weather this storm and rid yourself of depression—perhaps forever.

Chapter Two

SYMPTOMS AND DIAGNOSIS OF DEPRESSION

What is the difference between "the blues" and depression?

"The blues" refers to normal, transient sadness that lasts a few hours or days, at most. While many people with normal sadness claim they are "depressed," they are not experiencing an abnormal mood disturbance that warrants professional attention. When mental health professionals use the word "depression," they mean clinical depression, which is abnormal. By definition, clinical depression is so severe or sustained that it becomes very difficult to function normally in important areas of life.

How can I evaluate the seriousness of my depression?

Degree of seriousness is a function of the intensity, duration, and number of symptoms. If you have two or three symptoms, and they don't interfere with your life, then your case is considered mild. If, on the other hand, you have had six symptoms for several weeks, and they are growing more intense, then your case is serious enough to meet the criteria for major depression. Monique knew she was seriously depressed at age twenty-six when her weight dropped to 113 pounds and she began to "dread going to sleep at night because of how I knew I would feel in the morning."

In general, the more disruptive your symptoms are to your lifestyle, the deeper your depression is considered to be. You can evaluate all your symptoms as a whole, but it may be easier to examine symptom categories one at a time—bearing in mind that clinical depression always expresses itself through multiple symptoms, not just one.

Consider insomnia, which is extremely common in depression. There are four kinds of insomnia: difficulty falling asleep (primary insomnia), waking up repeatedly during the night (secondary insomnia), waking up earlier than usual (tertiary insomnia), and oversleeping (hypersomnia). A mildly depressed individual might have only primary insomnia, in addition to feeling sad. As the depression deepens, secondary and tertiary insomnia also set in. Clearly, it is far more difficult to function during the day if you are plagued by three forms of insomnia at night.

Another approach to determine the depth of your depression is to examine how all your symptoms are interfering with your quality of life and basic activities. Looking at all your symptoms as a whole, ask yourself, "To what degree is my depression adversely affecting my work, leisure time, and relationships?" or, "On a scale of zero to ten, with ten representing the best I have ever felt, how do I feel right now?" If you answer seven or eight, your depression is probably mild. Five or six might indicate a moderate degree of depression, and one to three suggests your depression is severe. Rating your own mood is hardly scientific, but it can give you a subjective sense of where you stand. Repeating this exercise once a month after you start treatment can help you and your therapist gauge your progress.

A more scientific way to quantify depression severity is to complete one of the "depression scales" used by some psychotherapists. These scales, such as the Beck Depression Inventory and Hamilton Rating Scale for Depression, have no right or wrong answers; they are evaluation tools. The Beck Inventory is a self-rating scale that concentrates on negative thinking patterns. It presents twenty-one statements, such as "I am disgusted with myself," and "I hate myself," which you rate from 0 to 3 based on how you are feeling at the time. The Hamilton Scale is a semistructured interview administered by your therapist. You are asked about various depressive symptoms, such as changes in your sleeping patterns and mood, and your answers are rated. The Hamilton Scale is widely used but has been criticized for overemphasizing the biological causes of depression. It should probably be coupled with at least one other depression scale to provide a more balanced assessment of your mood.

Do women and men experience or express their depression symptoms differently?

There are some gender differences, but they are driven mostly by culture and socialization. In general, men experience their depressions more cognitively—how it affects their view of the world and themselves. Women tend to express their depression more emotionally; they talk about what they feel more than what they think.

The starkest gender difference is the propensity to report depression. Despite the male celebrities who have gone public about their depression—including

Academy Award winner Rod Steiger and football player Earl Campbell—the disorder is still widely perceived as a weakness or character flaw, particularly by men. Depressed women, therefore, are far more likely to seek treatment, while men are more likely to suffer in silence.

Can depression cause psychosomatic illnesses?

Yes. In some cases, psychosomatic illness is considered "masked depression." A psychosomatic illness is any physical symptom that can be attributed to a mental, rather than a physical, cause. Psychosomatic symptoms most commonly occur among people who have trouble putting their feelings into words. Their mood disturbances are expressed through physical sensations or perceived ailments, such as headaches or stomachaches. Physical exams and laboratory tests show no medical reasons for these complaints. A function of a person's psychology and physiology, psychosomatic illness affects depressed men and women equally. You may hear a doctor refer to a psychosomatic illness as a "psychophysiological disorder."

How many different kinds of depression are there?

There are a half-dozen major categories and numerous subcategories that are used in the diagnosis of depression and bipolar disorder (manic depression). Some of the terms are technical, and knowing them probably won't affect your recovery. Still, it helps to be familiar with some of the diagnostic terminology your therapist may use to describe your condition to you or to your health insurance provider.

All forms of depression are called "mood disorders." Anyone who has experienced at least one "major depressive episode" is said to suffer from "major depressive disorder." If depression and mania occur simultaneously, it is called a "mixed episode." Chronic mild depression is known as dysthymia. Then there are depressions caused by a general medical condition or by substance abuse. Bipolar disorder can take several different forms.

To fine-tune your diagnosis, your therapist may use "specifiers" (specific features) to describe your most recent mood episode. Some of the specifiers are: postpartum onset, melancholic features; mild, moderate, and severe depression without psychotic features; and severe depression with psychotic features. Whether your latest depressive episode is in partial or full remission will also be noted. Additionally, there are specifiers to describe the course of recurrent depressive episodes. These include "seasonal pattern" of depressed moods that occur in the winter months, and "rapid cycling," which includes frequent manic or depressive symptoms, which may or may not alternate with each other, in a short space of time.

What is the difference between a major depressive "disorder" and a major depressive "episode"?

Major depressive "disorder" is a generic term for all the depressive illnesses. If you have a single depressive episode, you are diagnosed as having "major depressive disorder." If you have more than one episode, the diagnosis is changed to "recurrent major depressive disorder."

What constitutes a major depressive episode?

The most important feature of a major depressive episode is feeling empty, sad, or otherwise depressed or having a markedly diminished interest or pleasure in nearly all activities for at least two weeks, according to *DSM-IV*. To qualify for this diagnosis, *DSM-IV* states, you must also have four or more of the following other symptoms:

1. Losing or gaining more than 5 percent of your body weight in a month (without dieting).
2. Insomnia or hypersomnia nearly every day.
3. Visible "psychomotor agitation" (extreme nervousness) or "psychomotor retardation" (being slowed down) nearly every day.
4. Fatigue or loss of energy nearly every day.
5. Feelings of worthlessness or excessive inappropriate guilt nearly every day.
6. Trouble thinking or concentrating, or indecisiveness, nearly every day.
7. Recurrent thoughts about death, recurrent suicidal fantasies without a specific plan, a specific plan for committing suicide, or an actual suicide attempt.*

In order to meet the criteria for a major depressive episode, your symptoms cannot be attributable to bereavement. And your symptoms must cause significant impairment or distress in social settings, at work, or in other important areas of life.

Does the severity of depression symptoms change from morning to night?

Severely depressed people usually feel worse in the morning than they do at night. In lesser depressions, the converse is usually true.

*Reprinted with permission from the *Diagnostic and Statistical Manual of Mental Disorders,* Fourth Edition. Copyright 1994 American Psychiatric Association.

What is a typical day like for someone in the throes of a major depressive episode?

If the person is fortunate enough to have fallen asleep the night before, she probably wakes up early, before the dawn, and can't get back to sleep. The darkness of her mood matches the darkness outside her window. Her body feels heavy, as though there were weights tied to her limbs. She is lethargic. Her mouth is dry. Her senses are dulled. Her thoughts are pessimistic.

Eventually, she manages to drag herself out of bed, shower, and dress. She makes her way to the kitchen but has little interest in food and lacks the physical and emotional energy to cook. Nothing smells good, tastes good, or feels good. Negative events make her cry, so she doesn't read the newspaper anymore. She has little interest in taking care of her children and grows irritable as she goes through the motions of getting them ready for school. She is loath to drive the carpool and catch the commuter train. She considers calling in sick, as she had done the previous week when she couldn't motivate herself to get out of bed. But she changes her mind because she is afraid of losing her job.

When she arrives at her office, she has difficulty concentrating on work and develops a headache. She doesn't want to see other people because she feels inadequate, ineffectual, and guilty about not doing what's expected of her. This feeds her pervasive sense of anxiety. She thinks about dead relatives and wonders what it's like to be dead. At the end of the workday, she forgets to pick up her kids from a playmate's house. She doesn't want to cook or eat dinner. She regrets making plans to see friends over the weekend. After dinner, activities that used to give her pleasure—surfing the Internet, reading a good book, helping her kids with homework, watching a sitcom, listening to classical music, making love with her husband—no longer interest her. She looks forward only to crawling back into bed and shutting out the world.

The above scenario is a relatively extreme case. Usually, depression lifts or at least wanes during the course of the day. You may have a burst of pleasure or interest in something, such as a meal. This can lull you into the false belief that your depression is ending—until you wake up feeling lousy again the next day. Depression symptoms do not follow a smooth curve.

Do the symptoms of a major depressive episode come on gradually, or do they hit all at once?

In most cases, the onset of symptoms is insidious; they unfold over the course of weeks or months. In some cases, there's an acute precipitant, such as the loss of a job, that triggers the episode to begin rather suddenly. But more often than not, there is an amalgam of events and some kind of psychological and physiological reaction to those events, which gradually set a depressive episode in motion.

Are depression symptoms different if the disorder stems from a drug side effect or drug interaction, or from an underlying illness?

In general, depression is depression, regardless of the source. Sometimes, there are subtle hints that illness or medication is the culprit, such as being overly withdrawn and "flat," even for a clinically depressed person. If your mood is depressed because of a thyroid deficiency, you will have many of the classic depression symptoms, but rarely agitation. You will

probably have dry skin (which can also be a side effect of medication), and your reflexes will be slug-
gish. If your depression is being caused by alcoholism,
you may have an elevated liver function and tremors.
Only by looking at the full spectrum of symptoms
and doing appropriate blood work can a proper diagnosis be made. This often requires a good collaboration between the patient, therapist, and internist.

**I feel very irritable, which makes me snap at people,
especially those closest to me. Could this be a
symptom of depression?**

Definitely. People tend to think about depression
only as a state of sadness, but if you look at the criteria for a major depression, irritability is there. Of
course, irritability can also be a personality trait or
symptomatic of other mood disorders, such as anxiety, which is discussed in another book in this series,
If You Think You Have Panic Disorder. If you were
not an irritable person before your depression set in,
then your irritability is probably a symptom of depression. In clinically depressed children and adolescents, irritability and restlessness are often the
predominant features.

**Do recurrent episodes of major depression vary
in severity?**

Recurrent episodes sometimes worsen as people get
older. The severity of recurring episodes largely depends on your psychology and previous treatment, if
any. If you were effectively treated during your first
depressive episode, you will probably never experience depression in such a negative way again. For
one thing, you will understand what is happening to
you. You will know which form of treatment works

for you. You will know a good therapist and probably won't wait as long to get treated. Even if you have moved from Chicago to St. Louis since your initial episode, you now know how to look for a qualified therapist because you've been through the search process before.

Do depressed people differ in their perceptions of or reactions to their symptoms?

Yes. In many respects, the psychological pain of depression is analogous to physical pain. Both can be difficult to describe in words. And everyone has a different pain threshold.

For example, some people never donate blood because they cannot tolerate a needle in their arm. Others feel nothing when the needle is inserted. Likewise, some people can function at a remarkably high level despite their persistently dark mood. Others fall apart. Varying sensitivities to depression become clear when you consider how severely depressed people are when they walk into a therapist's office for the first time. Some patients come in prematurely, before their sad mood reaches a clinical stage. Others have been clinically depressed for more than a year or have attempted suicide. Then there are those who seek treatment at the most appropriate moment— when their symptoms have begun to damage their quality of life.

How do episodes of major depressive disorder vary from person to person?

Some people experience a single episode of depression and never have to face it again. Others experience several isolated episodes of major depression separated by many symptom-free years. In others, depressive episodes occur in clusters. Some people never quite recover from one major depressive episode before sinking into the next.

The frequency of depressive episodes may or may not increase as a person gets older. However, the more major depressive episodes you have, the higher your risk for future episodes. Research has shown that a person who has had two episodes of major depression has a 70 percent risk for a third episode, and those who have had a third have a 90 percent chance for a fourth.

How can I tell if I have dysthymia?

If you have been continually sad or "down in the dumps" (but not severely depressed or suicidal) for two or more years, then you probably have dysthymia, also known as dysthymic disorder. Children may be diagnosed with dysthymia if they are in a chronically depressed or irritable mood for at least one year. In addition to chronic depression, you must have at least two of the following additional symptoms to meet diagnostic criteria for dysthymia: poor appetite or overeating, sleep disturbance (insomnia or hypersomnia), low energy or fatigue, low self-esteem, poor concentration or difficulty making decisions, and feelings of hopelessness.

Some dysthymia sufferers put themselves down a lot; they may consider themselves "uninteresting" or "incapable" people. They seldom seek professional help, because they have been living with dysthymia for so long that the symptoms feel "normal." As with major depressive symptoms, dysthymic symptoms often creep up on a person. It is not unusual for symptoms to begin in childhood, adolescence, or young adulthood. Overall, about six percent of Americans will become dysthymic sometime during their life.

Is it common for people with dysthymia to also have major depressive episodes?

About one in ten people diagnosed with dysthymia will also suffer at least one major depressive episode. If the episode overlaps with the dysthymic period, the phenomenon is called "double depression." Double depression can be difficult to diagnose, because symptoms of the two disorders are similar.

What are the symptoms of a mixed mood episode?

This serious but rare mental disturbance is diagnosed when someone has symptoms of depression and mania simultaneously. For example, someone feels sad emotionally but has grandiose notions when thinking about a business decision. Or the person has boundless energy but no interest in channeling it into something he or she previously enjoyed. Extreme irritability is the hallmark of a mixed mood disorder. Victims of mixed mood episodes are sometimes referred to as "grumpy manics."

Is there such thing as premenstrual depression?

Yes, its technical name is premenstrual dysphoric disorder. It is diagnosed if you regularly experience a remarkably depressed mood, marked anxiety, and decreased interest in activities during the week leading up to menses, and these symptoms go away within a few days after the onset of your period. Symptoms must be present during most menstrual cycles during the past year and be absent for at least one week after your period ends. Additionally, your

symptoms must interfere with work, school, or other
activities to qualify for this diagnosis.

What other forms of depression are there?

• *Minor depressive disorder.* This refers to episodes
of at least two weeks of depressive symptoms but
with fewer than the five items required for major depressive disorder.

• *Severe depression with psychotic features.* This
means the depressed patient is having delusions or hallucinations, usually with depressive themes. For instance, the patient may feel inappropriately guilty for
someone else's misfortune, or hear disembodied voices
that tell the patient he or she is worthless. Hallucinations in severely depressed people are usually transient.

• *Recurrent brief depressive disorder.* Depressive
episodes lasting from two days up to two weeks, occurring at least once a month for twelve months but
not associated with the menstrual cycle.

• *Major depression with melancholic features.* This
diagnosis may be used when a depressed patient's
mood fails to brighten, even briefly, when something
good happens. Three of the following symptoms
must also be present: "a distinct quality of the depressed mood (i.e., it feels distinctly different from
the kind of feeling experienced after the death of a
loved one); depression is regularly worse in the morning, early morning awakening (at least two hours before usual), marked psychomotor retardation or
agitation, significant anorexia or weight loss, excessive or inappropriate guilt," according to *DSM-IV.*

• *Atypical depression.* Instead of waking up too
early and having no appetite, as happens in classic

depression, these patients tend to oversleep and overeat. Their moods get progressively worse, instead of better, during the day.

• *Seasonal affective disorder,* which is distinguished by depressive symptoms that begin in the late fall or winter and disappear in the spring and summer.

• *Postpartum depression.* This refers to major depression that occurs two weeks to one year after giving birth, with an average of three to six months after delivery. As many as 15 percent of mothers experience postpartum depression (PPD).

• *Adjustment disorder with depressed mood.* Feelings of tearfulness, sadness, or hopelessness that are triggered by a life change, such as going away to college or switching jobs.

What are the symptoms of postpartum depression?

There are a multitude of symptoms associated with PPD. They include anxiety; difficulty making decisions; fear of being alone; forgetfulness; confusion; lack of interest in activities you previously enjoyed; significant appetite changes; sleep problems; crying for no apparent reason; difficulty touching or caring for the baby; regrets over having the baby; hating your husband, baby, or yourself; hostility; tantrums; nervousness; feeling out of control; breast-feeding problems; feelings of hopelessness; bodily aches; and panic attacks. Many PPD sufferers feel trapped and want to leave their family. Some want to hurt themselves or the baby. Women with PPD are at high risk for drug or alcohol abuse.

You need only have a handful of symptoms to qualify for a diagnosis of PPD, but symptoms must have begun within the first twelve months of giving birth.

What is the difference between postpartum blues and postpartum depression?

Blues last up to four days before the tearfulness and sadness subside. The blues usually dissipate without outside intervention beyond the support of family and friends. The blues are considered normal and affect one half to 80 percent of women within the first five days after delivery.

PPD is a much bigger problem. Its symptoms are the same as major depression and last at least two weeks. The risk of PPD is higher among women with a personal or family history of depression or other psychiatric problems.

What are the symptoms of bipolar disorder?

People with bipolar disorder alternate between clinical depression and elated or euphoric moods (mania). The manic phase of this illness can produce high levels of energy, unusual social behaviors, poor judgment, insomnia, and racing thoughts. Each mood can last anywhere from a few hours to several months before switching to the opposite mood. Every time Belinda becomes depressed, she initiates heated arguments with her husband. During her manic phases, she becomes warm and passionate at home and more productive than usual at work. Like most bipolar patients, Belinda also has periods when her moods are normal. Bipolar disorder affects 0.4 to 1.6 percent of the population; an estimated 10 percent of depressed people experience manic episodes.

Owing to the various textures of bipolar disorder,

the mental health community now classifies manic-depressives into various subcategories:

• Bipolar I disorder, which is marked by significant manic episodes and quiet depressions.

• Bipolar II disorder, for those with more significant depressions and milder manic periods.

• Bipolar III disorder, an unofficial diagnosis given when the patient is generally depressed but becomes manic when taking antidepressant medication. A family history of depression is also present in cases of bipolar III disorder.

• *Cyclothymic (SI-clo-THI-mic) disorder,* in which the patient experiences several manic-depressive cycles over a course of at least two years. (The duration must be at least one year in children and adolescents.) During this period, the patient goes no more than two months without symptoms, and the symptoms are severe enough to produce significant distress or impairment. If the patient suffers more than one depressive and manic cycle within a week, the disorder is called "rapid cycling." So-called "ultra-rapid cycling" occurs when the patient cycles from sadness to irritability up to several times a day. Symptoms generally include agitation, appetite changes, psychosis (losing touch with reality), and thoughts of suicide. Some patients are so disabled or endangered by this condition that they need to be hospitalized. Fortunately, this condition is very rare.

How does bereavement differ from depression?

Bereavement is a normal grief reaction to the loss, usually through death, of someone close to you. Bereavement and depression do share some of the same symptoms, such as sadness, insomnia, and weight loss. However, bereavement lasts an average of two months compared to clinical depression, which lasts an average of six months if untreated. Antidepressants often block symptoms in clinically depressed people. If you were to take antidepressants during a normal bereavement period, there would be no beneficial effect.

Sometimes, loss of a loved one triggers a depressive episode. Thoughts such as "I am really going to miss this person. Life will never be the same" are part of the normal grief process. If, on the other hand, you think, "I cannot go on living without this person. Life isn't worth living anymore," you may be clinically depressed in addition to being bereaved. Other indications that your grief reaction is abnormal include a morbid preoccupation with feelings of worthlessness, significant and prolonged inability to function, and guilt that is unrelated to your loved one's death, according to *DSM-IV*. Remember, the duration of normal bereavement may be connected to the type of relationship you had with the person you lost. If you are concerned that your grief is turning into clinical depression, you should probably talk to your rabbi or pastor, a trained grief counselor, or a mental health practitioner.

DIAGNOSING DEPRESSION

How is depression diagnosed?

As you now know, there is a whole litany of symptoms associated with clinical depression. Your therapist's job is to ascertain what your symptoms are, decide whether they are indicative of a depressed mood, and determine whether the symptoms have persisted long enough to justify a diagnosis of depression. By looking at all your symptoms, the therapist must also determine whether there are confounding factors, such as postpartum depression, depression superimposed on a personality disorder, depression related to a medical disorder, or depression induced by drugs—legal or illegal.

Clearly, then, a thorough account of your past and present symptoms—your "history"—is by far the most valid diagnostic tool. Your therapist will consider, among other things, when your symptoms began, whether your symptoms have plagued you before, whether you have any medical illnesses that can produce depression, and whether any blood relatives have suffered depression. If a family member has been successfully treated for depression, the therapist will probably ask what kind of treatment was used. A good therapist will also ask you about specific symptoms that you did not mention. You might be asked, for example, if your appetite has changed or if you are having trouble sleeping.

Can my cultural, religious, or ethnic background influence how I experience or communicate my depressive symptoms?

Yes. In some countries and ethnic groups, depression may be experienced largely through physical symptoms rather than sadness or lack or interest. For instance, Hispanic people might complain of "nervousness"; Asians might speak of lassitude and fatigue. People who practice their religion in a rigid manner may experience more guilt in their depression. They may believe, for example, that they are not living up to the expectations of their religious leader, themselves, or God.

Are some races or cultures more prone to depression than others?

No. Depression and other mood disorders are color- and culture-blind.

How long is the average patient depressed before he or she seeks professional help?

The average person is depressed for three or four months before making an appointment with a therapist. It is not unusual for these people to have a history of untreated depression. As pointed out in Chapter One, an estimated 80 percent of clinically depressed people never seek help, and 50 percent never realize that they are depressed in the first place.

If people are depressed that long, what finally motivates them to get help?

Some hear about a new antidepressant and want to give it a try. Others are responding to a crisis that grew out of their depression, such as their spouse threatening to leave them or their boss threatening to fire them if they don't get help. An item in the news, such as a famous person being successfully treated for depression, can inspire someone to get help. Others find they are so debilitated that they have withdrawn socially and can no longer function optimally at work, home, or school. Occasionally, someone attempts suicide or otherwise "hits bottom" and acknowledges that he or she needs professional help.

Will I need to undergo any blood tests prior to my initial consultation with a mental health professional?

When you call to make your first appointment, the therapist, secretary, or office manager will ask you to state in a general sense why you want to be seen. If there is a potential that you are depressed, you may be asked to undergo several blood tests prior to your consultation. These blood tests do not diagnose depression; they test for a variety of medical conditions that can mimic depression. It is also important to rule out certain illnesses if antidepressants are to be used. The tests generally include:

- Complete blood count (CBC), which tests for anemia;
- "Chem screen" to assess liver and kidney function;
- "Electrolytes" (part of the chem screen) to measure the levels of potassium, sodium, and calcium in your blood. This may rule out various metabolic causes of depression.
- "Thyroid profile," particularly a thyroid stimulating hormone (TSH) test, which can detect an underactive or overactive thyroid gland.

Depending on where you live, your blood may also be screened for Lyme disease, a tick-borne illness that sometimes causes psychiatric symptoms, especially depression. Lyme disease is most prevalent in the northeastern United States but has also been reported in other regions and other countries.

In addition to blood tests, an electrocardiogram (EKG) may be ordered to make sure your heart is strong enough to withstand certain antidepressants, should they be indicated.

Will the subject of suicide come up during my first consultation?

It ought to. Before broaching the issue (if you don't bring it up yourself), your therapist will probably wait until some rapport has been established. But anytime depression is suspected, questions about suicide are essential in helping to determine the severity of your disorder. According to the American Psychological Association, studies have found that 75 percent of individuals who commit suicide have had a previous attempt and that users of university counseling services are five to six times more likely than nonusers to commit suicide.

The first suicide question will probably be something like "Have you had thoughts of harming yourself?" If you answer in the affirmative, your therapist must assess how lethal your situation is. You may be asked: "Have you ever attempted to harm or kill yourself?" and "Has anyone in your family ever committed or attempted suicide?" Clearly, answering "yes" to either or both of those questions indicates a very serious problem.

The therapist also needs to find out whether you have a formal suicide plan versus some vague notion of not wanting to live. Do you have control over your suicidal thoughts? Do you expect to act on them? If you profess to having no control over your suicidal thoughts, the therapist might admit you to a hospital right away, for your own protection. If you do have control over your suicidal thoughts, the therapist will want to know if that sense of control is a) reassuring, or b) upsetting to you. Thinking about suicide in a controlled manner, and feeling reassured by that control, has gotten depressed people through many a dark night. The reason is that severely depressed people often feel trapped, hopeless, and helpless. Sometimes, passive suicidal thoughts such as "I don't care if I get hit by a truck," or "I wouldn't mind dying to get relief from all this pain," serve as a metaphorical door out of a room with no other doors. There is a wide gulf between thought and action, and merely thinking about suicide doesn't necessarily mean you belong in a psychiatric hospital.

I feel frightened and embarrassed by my thoughts of suicide. How can I discuss something so personal with a stranger?

Therapists are accustomed to these kinds of discussions; they should not act shocked or judgmental. Most of the time, suicidal patients are relieved, even comforted, when their therapist begins asking them about their suicidal thoughts. These provocative questions can mark a turning point in therapy and help build trust between you and your therapist.

Are any medical tests used to diagnose depression?

At the moment, there are no reliable blood tests for depression. Decades ago, blood tests for depression, such as the dexamethasone suppression test, were developed. These fell out of favor because they turned out to be unreliable.

There are two brain-imaging scans—positron emission tomography (PET) and single photon emission computed tomography (SPECT)—that show glucose metabolism in certain parts of the brain. These tests are used by researchers and would be helpful diagnostic tools, but they are too costly to be used routinely. They aren't really needed anyway, because depression is a fairly easy diagnosis to make based on your symptoms and mental health history.

Can the therapist tell from my facial expressions or demeanor whether I am depressed?

Yes. Some depressed individuals are very withdrawn; they sit in the therapist's office like a piece of clay. Others are visibly agitated and can't seem to sit still. They may even pace around the room. A furrowed brow or a flat or downward expression are other indicators of depression, as is crying. Some patients would like to cry but cannot because they are too cut off from their feelings.

Will my therapist want to talk to my spouse or other family members?

That depends on your situation. Your therapist may invite your husband or wife to one or more therapy sessions if he or she is a major source of your depression, or a major source of support. Otherwise, most therapists might talk to a spouse or other close relative only if you seem to be holding back something important in therapy. In most circumstances, the therapist should get your permission before speaking to any of your family members.

Most therapists would answer a telephone call from a relative only if there was an emergency, or if the relative is somehow responsible for your welfare and you have already given consent for this communication. The therapist should not take a call from your uncle Joe in Toledo who is merely curious about your condition.

With adolescents, most therapists want to speak with the parents or guardian at least once, but only with the patient's knowledge and often in the patient's presence. The therapist should never break a youngster's confidence unless the depression appears to be life-threatening.

Can depression be diagnosed in one session?

Yes, especially when the therapist has results of your blood tests to rule out medical conditions that can mimic depression.

Is depression ever missed or misdiagnosed?

Unfortunately, the answer is yes. Incompetence, lack of experience, and lack of training exist within the mental health profession. There are also professional blind spots; some therapists can't recognize depression when they see it. Certain therapists are simply uncomfortable dealing with depressed people and therefore miss the symptoms.

Misdiagnosis is another significant problem. A patient who paces throughout an initial consultation might be misdiagnosed as having an anxiety disorder when it is really an anxiety symptom of depression. A delusional patient may be diagnosed with schizophrenia when the real problem is delusional depression. Dysthymia can be misdiagnosed as a personality disorder. A new mother may be told she has the "baby blues" when her symptoms have exceeded the blues in both duration and intensity. Misdiagnosis can also occur when the depression is extremely complicated or the patient provides a poor or unreliable history. Mistakes are made even by the most seasoned therapist.

Then there is the myriad of medical conditions—Parkinson's disease, Alzheimer's disease, encephalitis and other infectious diseases, blood clots in the brain (stroke)—that can leave a person clinically depressed. If you had stroke, for example, and became depressed as a result, a practitioner might say, "Who wouldn't be depressed after having a stroke?" and send you on your way. Studies show that up to 60 percent of stroke patients—especially when the stroke occurred in the left anterior part of the brain—become clinically depressed and respond remarkably well to antidepressants. Many cancer patients also can benefit from depression treatment. Just because there is an obvious, external cause for depression, that doesn't necessarily mean the depression should be ignored. Refusing to treat depression in medically ill patients is tantamount to refusing to cast a fractured leg because your doctor knows your leg broke in a tumble down the stairs.

Do some patients fake being depressed just so they can get their hands on Prozac or another antidepressant?

There are a certain number of drug-seeking patients. In most cases, though, these patients claim they are suffering from anxiety or insomnia and are looking for sleeping pills or tranquilizers. Some pretend to be depressed because they are trying to get out of work or other responsibilities. These behaviors are known as "secondary gain" tactics, and they can be conscious or unconscious. An astute therapist usually will recognize these cons for what they are.

I visited a psychiatrist who said I wasn't clinically depressed. I disagree. Should I find another doctor?

You are always free to get a second opinion. If two or more therapists reach the same conclusion, however, it is fair to assume they are on the right track.

A common example is the active alcoholic whose therapist refuses to prescribe an antidepressant or start psychotherapy until the patient is abstinent. The therapist knows that certain antidepressants should not be mixed with alcohol and that psychotherapy is often ineffective with active alcoholics. Moreover, the therapist may want to find out if the patient's depression lifts on its own when the drinking stops. The patient disagrees with that assessment and seeks out another therapist.

The bottom line is this: Regardless of whether you agree with your therapist's assessment, the assessment should make sense to you. If not, find another mental health specialist (Chapter Four).

Chapter Three

CAUSES OF DEPRESSION

Why is depression so widespread?

Nobody knows. The enormous scope of depression probably has something to do with our biochemistry, psychology, and environment. Healthy functioning of our brains depends on the normal interplay of a variety of chemicals, known as "neurotransmitters," which help facilitate communication among brain cells. A slight abnormality of certain neurotransmitters may be all it takes to precipitate a depressive episode, or to predispose someone to depression.

Beyond the biochemical causes, there are a multitude of psychological factors, such as low self-esteem and unconscious conflicts, which are very common and can lead to a depressed mood in susceptible people. There are also many potential external triggers for depression—job loss and divorce, for example—that occur too often in our society.

Which brain chemicals are abnormal in depressed people?

There are three primary neurotransmitters, or brain chemicals, known to be related to depression. Serotonin is probably the most important one. It is believed to be involved in controlling mood and states of consciousness. Next is norepinephrine, a relative of adrenaline, the so-called "fight-or-flight" hormone. Norepinephrine is secreted by certain nerve endings as well as by the adrenal glands. The third brain chemical involved in depression is dopamine. Like norepinephrine, dopamine is a hormonelike substance that plays a variety of roles in the brain. Dopamine imbalances have been associated with Parkinson's disease, schizophrenia, and alcoholism, as well as depression.

How do these neurotransmitters control mood?

Twenty years ago, it was thought that depression meant there was simply a decrease in the levels of serotonin, norepinephrine, and dopamine in the brain. Researchers now realize that depression is far more complex. The normal and abnormal interplay among serotonin, norepinephrine, and dopamine are only beginning to be understood.

According to current theories, serotonin, norepinephrine, and dopamine are involved in the functioning of "mood centers." Mood centers are believed to be collections of different neurons spread throughout the brain. When the mood centers are functioning well, it means the neurotransmitters are working in synch, facilitating smooth communication among and between the brain cells involved in controlling mood. When the neurotransmitters are malfunctioning in ways not completely understood, depression sets in. If there was merely a deficiency of neurotransmitters, depression could be cured overnight by adding more neurotransmitters through medication. This, however, is not the case. It takes time, up to six weeks, for antidepressants to normalize neurotransmitter activity.

A close analogy is an arrhythmia in the heart. The heart is still beating, but its rhythm is too fast and out of synch. Blood is not being circulated efficiently. Over time, heart medications serve to "downregulate" the arrhythmia—slow down and normalize the heart rate. In the brain, antidepressants "downregulate" or "upregulate" the brain cells in the mood centers, which are presumably firing too fast or too slowly and causing depression.

Are there any theories as to what causes neurotransmitter abnormalities?

The more severe the depression, the more it appears to be genetically related. For example, your risk for major depressive disorder is one and a half to three times that of the general population if your parent or sibling has the disorder. In particular, having a certain genetic component in the "serotonin transporter gene" may predispose some people to major depression, according to one recent study in *The Lancet*, a respected medical journal published in Britain.

Oftentimes, depression lies dormant until the level of stress in a person's life reaches a critical mass. According to this "physiological stress theory," when the brain is overloaded physiologically, psychologically, or sociologically, whatever mental disorder a person may have expresses itself. For example, if you are genetically predisposed to depression and suffer the loss of a loved one, a job, self-esteem, or you experience extreme isolation, excessive work, or another stressful situation, then you are more likely to become depressed. If you were predisposed to having phobias or anxiety attacks, then either of those disorders would occur as a result of the same stressful situation.

The same goes for cancer or heart disease. Certain people inherit genes that code for cancer or heart disease, but the expression of those genes is partially dependent on lifestyle factors, such as smoking and diet. That doesn't mean people can control whether they develop cancer, heart disease, or depression. In each case, there is a confluence of causes—some you can influence, some you cannot.

Are there other theories about the biological causes of depression?

The abnormal metabolism of certain electrolytes in the neurons have been studied as a possible contributing factor in depression, especially bipolar disorders. Specifically, there is some evidence to support the hypothesis that excess sodium moves into the neurons during mood disorder episodes and that sodium balance is restored during recovery. Abnormalities in biological rhythms, particularly dream-phase sleep, also are being investigated as possible causes of depression and bipolar disorder.

Evolutionary psychologists have another theory: We are genetically programmed to thrive in a hunter-gatherer society. Anthropologists tell us that hunter-gatherers were an intensely social species, with members of large clans looking out for each other's children and everyone depending on each other for their day-to-day survival. Today, as many as one out of four Americans live alone. Cars, personal computers, and television sets isolate us from our neighbors. It is this mismatch between our genetic makeup and the modern world that could be a source of our depression, theorists told *Time* magazine in an August 1995 article. As possible proof, evolutionary psychologists point to the primitive tribes of today, such as the Kaluli of New Guinea and the !Kung hunter-gatherers in Africa, where clinical depression does not seem to exist.

People tell me my depression is all in my head, that I should just pick myself up by my bootstraps and snap out of it. Are they right?

Strictly speaking, the first part of that statement is correct: Depression *is* all in your head—your brain has sole province over your mood. If you can elevate your mood without any help, you probably never had clinical depression. You were experiencing the normal feelings of sadness. With major depression, you can probably get yourself through a particular day or particular experience without letting on that you are depressed. But "snapping out" of a major depressive episode through sheer force of will is virtually impossible. Comments such as "pick yourself up by your bootstraps" are usually made out of fear, denial, ignorance, or false stereotypes. No one would think of asking a diabetic or schizophrenic to cure themselves without professional help.

My mother suffered depressive episodes throughout most of her life. Does this increase my risk for depression?

Absolutely. In fact, a family history of depression may make your risk two or three times that of the general population. The most convincing evidence for this comes from studies of twins done in the late 1980s. If one identical twin became depressed, so did the other one in 65 to 75 percent of cases. This compares to a 14 to 19 percent correlation rate for fraternal twins. These numbers are consistent even among twins who were separated at birth. Research has shown that relatives who suffer from depression also tend to respond to the same antidepressants. Scientists have begun to isolate markers around different genes that appear to be responsible for depressive illnesses, with the ultimate goal of developing a cure. Cloning of laboratory animals bred for depression is expected to advance the search for these genes considerably.

How old is the average depressed patient?

In most cases, the initial episode of clinical depression occurs in the twenties or thirties. No one knows why this is the case, although there may be a physiological reason. There also may be some sociological factors. Formal education for many people doesn't end until age twenty-one, and in some cases, thirty or older. Finishing college or graduate school is one of the milestones known to trigger depression in vulnerable individuals.

Looking at depression over many decades, the age of onset has gotten younger. In the 1920s and '30s, adolescent depression seemed very rare, and depression in children was unheard of. Today, adolescent depression seems very pervasive, and there is a lot more childhood depression. For girls, this could be a mirror image of menses onset, which is also shifting to earlier ages. It may be that parents and pediatricians are more sophisticated when it comes to recognizing depression in young people. It may be that there are more pressures on today's children and teens to achieve academically and socially. There is also more drug abuse among young people, which can trigger or mask clinical depression.

Why is teenage depression so pervasive?

Teenagers encounter a mother lode of stresses as they approach adulthood, any one of which can affect their mood: changing bodies, peer pressure, learning to drive perhaps before they are emotionally ready for the responsibility, drugs, trying to separate from their parents yet still being dependent on them. Despite all that, adolescence is *not* a statistically peak time for clinical depression. Periodic moodiness and brooding are considered normal during the preteen and teen years. Teenage depression tends to get a lot of publicity, probably because of the drama and poignancy of teen suicide. Adolescents tend to be impulsive and action-oriented, which also can contribute to suicide in this age group.

What causes postpartum depression?

As with other forms of depression, PPD is believed to have multiple causes. For one thing, there is a dramatic shift in the ratio of estrogen and progesterone during pregnancy, and another shift after childbirth. These hormonal changes can wreak havoc on the emotions of women who are predisposed to depression. The stress of suddenly being responsible for a helpless baby is also thought to contribute to PPD, which affects 10 to 15 percent of women generally within three to six months after childbirth. The risk of postpartum depression is higher for women with a psychiatric history.

I became severely depressed after my miscarriage. How common is this?

One study found that 11 percent of 229 miscarrying women suffered an episode of major depressive disorder within six months after losing their pregnancy. That compared to a 4.3 percent depression rate among a control group of 230 women who were randomly selected for the study. Childless women who miscarried were almost five times more likely to become clinically depressed than miscarrying women who were already mothers. Seventy-two percent of postmiscarriage depressions began within the first month after pregnancy loss, according to the study in the February 5, 1997, *Journal of the American Medical Association*. The study also found that women with a history of depression were more likely to suffer a recurrence after miscarriage.

Can pregnancy cause depression?

Possibly. About one in ten women in this country suffer a major depressive episode during pregnancy. Risk factors for this include marital problems, a previous bout with depression, a family history of the disorder, and an unwanted pregnancy.

Do single people have an elevated risk for depression?

Unmarried people who are not in long-term, intimate relationships have a somewhat higher depression rate compared with married people. The lowest depression rates occur among happily married men. Single, elderly, white males and people in unhappy marriages suffer the highest rates of depression.

Are senior citizens especially vulnerable to depression?

People of advanced years certainly have an increased risk for depression. Part of the reason may have to do with diminishing levels and ratios of neurotransmitters. But there is also more loss in their lives. Senior citizens may face the loss of health, a spouse, and attractiveness in a culture that values a youthful appearance. Upon retirement, seniors may miss the prestige and status they enjoyed during their working years. This is where researcher Erik Erikson's concept of "ego integrity vs. ego despair" comes into play: those who can look back on their lives in a positive sense feel good; those who cannot feel a sense of despair, which can lead to clinical depression.

From a cultural standpoint, elderly Americans tend to get less respect and become more isolated in their supposed golden years—two more ingredients for depression.

Why are so many women affected by depression?

Women have more internal and external triggers for depression, particularly mild depressive states. Internally, women have a hormonal "feedback loop," which has been very well studied in depression. The loop begins with the hypothalamus, goes to the pituitary, then to the adrenal glands, then to the ovaries. As a result, changing levels of estrogen and progesterone throughout the menstrual cycle affect mood. Anyone who has experienced the emotional turmoil of premenstrual syndrome has had a taste of what this feedback loop is all about. Feeling blue just before your period, however, is not the same as clinical depression. In clinically depressed women, something in the hormonal feedback loop may be off kilter. In men, there is a similar feedback loop, but it includes the testes to a lesser degree. Thus, female sex hormones play a potentially significant role in depression, while male sex hormones appear to be less involved in mood control. Postpartum depression, by definition, affects women exclusively. And women have "a more precarious thyroid status (often associated with chronic and rapid-cycling mood episodes)," notes Hagop S. Akiskal, M.D., in a chapter on mood disorders in the *Comprehensive Textbook of Psychiatry/IV* (Williams and Wilkins, 1995).

Externally, there are extraordinary societal pressures on women that men generally escape. More than half of American mothers now work outside the home. Yet surveys show that women still shoulder the lion's share of housework, meal preparation, shopping, and childcare responsibilities. Women are also more likely than men to take on yet another burden, that of caregiver. According to a 1994 national survey, 81 percent of family caregivers are female. And 49 percent suffer from prolonged depression because of their caregiving experience, according to the survey by the National Family Caregivers Association of Kensington, Maryland. The association defines caregivers as family, friends, and neighbors who help loved ones who face chronic illness or disability. There are an estimated 25 million family caregivers nationwide.

In addition to stress at home, women generally have more stress in the workplace. They still earn less money than men for the same work, are far less likely to hold top corporate positions, and they confront sexual harassment on the job with much greater frequency. Back at home, women are far more likely than men to be victims of domestic violence.

Bulimia and anorexia are largely female problems, partly because of the emphasis our culture places on female thinness. Pity the overweight single woman scouring personal ads for a date. The vast majority of ads placed by men specify "thin" as a prerequisite.

From a sociological perspective, men are encouraged to express their aggression directly; women are taught to hold it in. In Freud's view, people who hold in their anger ultimately turn the anger in toward themselves. This can lead to a sense of helplessness and worthlessness, which are symptomatic of depression.

If women suffer from depression in greater numbers than men, why are the majority of suicides male?

The statistics are deceiving. It is true that the highest suicide rate in this country is among single, white elderly men. But the rate of suicide *attempts* among women is about twice that of men. Men are more successful in committing suicide because they tend to use more lethal methods—guns and cars—to kill themselves. Women are more likely to attempt a drug overdose, a less effective form of suicide.

What causes bipolar disorder?

As with unipolar depression, manic depression is a complex illness with no known cause. It is believed to stem from an abnormality in the brain's neurotransmitters, and there is evidence suggesting that bipolar disorder is hereditary. Bipolar disorder is rare, affecting about 0.4 to 1.6 percent of Western populations. It usually develops in late adolescence.

What are the most common external triggers of depression?

- Loneliness or isolation
- Chronic illness
- Financial difficulties

- Death of a loved one (or the anniversary of a loved one's death)
- Divorce or ending of a relationship
- Marriage or relationship problems
- Sexual, emotional, or physical abuse as a child or adult
- Involvement in a major disaster, war, or accident
- Long-term caregiving to a chronically ill loved one
- Retirement
- Surgery or childbirth
- Suicide of a friend or relative
- Chronic illness or chronic pain
- Joblessness
- Life transitions, such as moving or graduating

What, if anything, do all of these situations have in common?

All involve loss, be it tangible or intangible. Loss is the real centerpiece of depression.

Why do some people feel depressed after undergoing surgery?

There are several reasons for this. The first is general anesthesia, which is a central nervous system depressant. All drugs used to put patients to sleep during surgery are fat soluble, and the brain is mostly fat. So these drugs can linger in the brain tissue for days or weeks after an operation. Pain medication, which many people take postoperatively, is also a depressant.

Hospitalization can also trigger a depressive episode. You are away from your loved ones, confined to bed. You lack control and are dependent on others for your basic needs—all while being stressed out over your injury or illness. Then there is the reality of the surgery itself: What was removed? What was put in? Will the surgery affect your self-image or lifestyle?

Interestingly, most people who feel depressed after surgery don't quite fit the criteria for major depression. This diagnosis should not even be considered until several weeks after every trace of anesthesia and pain medication has been purged by the body. In most cases, seemingly depressed patients are having an inappropriate or excessive reaction to their surgery and don't need antidepressants. Rather, these patients often benefit from taking a stimulant, such as Ritalin (methylphenidate) or Dexedrine (amphetamine), which work right away. Antidepressants usually take several weeks to have an impact, and by then the postsurgical blues are usually gone. Stimulants are particularly effective in combating depression in hospital patients who have not necessarily undergone surgery, such as poststroke patients and cancer patients.

Unless they specialize in counseling hospital patients, doctors, including oncologists and even psychiatrists, are generally unaware of the benefits of stimulants. If you feel depressed after surgery or during a hospitalization, you probably won't get a stimulant unless you request one.

Is depression common among people with chronic diseases?

More than half of patients with chronic diseases experience clinical depression, according to a 1996 report in the *Journal of the American Medical Association.* Major depression, dysthymia, or adjustment disorder with depression are common in people with neurological diseases, including Parkinson's and dementia; cancer and diabetes.

Is there a connection between boredom and depression?

It has been said that boredom is one of the great psychological smoke screens. You might be bored simply because you are not interested in what's going on at the moment. You might be bored because you have exquisitely high intellectual or emotional needs, or you are narcissistic and need to be fed, nurtured, and entertained all the time. Or you may be bored because you are clinically depressed. Most people experiencing a major depression find it impossible to get excited over anything.

Are any medical conditions likely to cause depression?

Yes. Low thyroid hormone output, or hypothyroidism, is one of the most common medical illnesses that causes depression. Hypothyroidism affects about one percent of the adult population and is usually caused by the body developing antibodies that attack its own thyroid tissue. Low mood and low energy stemming from the underproduction of thyroid hormones often reverse themselves without antidepressants once the patient starts taking medication to compensate for their diminished thyroid output.

Anemia is another ailment that typically causes depression. There are several kinds of anemia, the most common of which is an iron deficiency stemming from a reduction in the amount of hemoglobin (oxygen-carrying pigment) in the blood. If you are depressed because you are anemic, eating iron-rich foods, taking iron supplements, or otherwise treating your condition should clear up your depression. Therapists and physicians should order blood tests to rule out both hypothyroidism and anemia in every patient complaining of depressive symptoms.

More rarely, depression is caused by a brain tumor or pancreatic cancer. Multiple sclerosis and other neurological conditions can also precipitate depression, as can stroke, high calcium or low calcium, hyperthyroidism (an overactive thyroid gland), and certain infections, including the flu and encephalitis. Even the common cold can get people's mood down because their brain chemistry is affected.

What is the relationship between stress and depression?

Consider some of life's stressors—death of a loved one, moving, divorce, unemployment, retirement. They all involve loss. Even the indescribable joy of becoming a first-time parent is tempered by the loss of freedom to come and go at will. It is loss, both real and symbolic, that is the great stressor in our lives.

Some people cope marvelously well with loss; others are devastated by it. Some people are happy to move away from their hometowns; others are crushed by not seeing their old friends and neighbors. Some retirees love their gold watch and can't wait to hit the golf course; others go into horrible tailspins of depression. Why loss triggers depression in some people but not in others remains a mystery.

Can any medications cause depression as a side effect?

Technically, any medication that crosses the "blood-brain barrier"—the magical area of the brain where some drugs get through and others don't—has the potential of causing depression. Of course, some drugs are more notorious than others. Valium, sleeping pills, and other tranquilizers and antianxiety drugs typically cause depression, especially with long-term use. Aldomet, used to treat high blood pressure, is also known to cause depression. In fact, almost all antihypertensives can cause depression, but the worst are the beta-blockers, which can cause significant depression. Calcium channel blockers constitute the only class of blood pressure drugs that probably don't cause depression. Certain antibiotics can also cause depression. If you are concerned about this side effect, consult your doctor or pharmacist.

What should I do if I must take one of these drugs to maintain my health?

If you are prone to depression or have a family history of the disorder, inform your doctor before beginning a new medication that you'll be taking for a long time. It may be possible to prescribe another drug. If there is no way around your dilemma, it is safe to take an antidepressant to treat a drug-induced depression. However, taking an antidepressant under these circumstances should always be a last resort.

Conversely, if you are depressed and taking medication to control a medical problem, tell your doctor or psychiatrist what you are taking. It may be that your depression is being caused by the drug and not by an inherent abnormality in your brain chemistry. In fact, you should always tell your doctor the name of any and all prescription and over-the-counter medications you are taking. It is possible that your depression is a result of a drug interaction and can be corrected by a medication switch.

Are certain personality types more likely than others to get depressed?

There are several personality types that seem to pre-dispose people to depression under the right set of circumstances. For example, when someone with a dependent personality loses a loved one or experiences the end of a relationship, that person is at high risk for depression. Another example would be someone with obsessive-compulsive or perfectionist traits who causes a car accident in which someone else gets hurt. These individuals would likely become depressed because they hold such a rigid view of themselves and the world and can be very unforgiving of their own mistakes. A third example would be a narcissistic person who experiences a loss or some kind of attack on his or her self-image. People with borderline personality disorder—who are typically unstable with regard to their relationships, self-image, and moods—would likely become depressed if they became involved in a quixotic, rocky relationship.

So, basically depression can occur when there is a match between certain personality styles and particular stressful situations.

What are some of the psychological causes of depression?

Loss of self-esteem is one of the most important psychological causes of depression. Your self-esteem can be diminished by real losses, such as divorce or unemployment, or by symbolic losses, such as loss of power, values, or identity. Unconscious conflicts can also precipitate a depressive episode. For example, you may yearn to move out of your parents' home but can't bring yourself to do it. Here, your conflict is between autonomy and dependence. You still feel tethered to your parents but are not consciously aware of this dependence.

Another psychological cause of depression is holding an excessively negative view of the world and relationships. If these people fall short of a particular goal, they expect to fail in all their pursuits. If a boyfriend breaks up with them, they feel unworthy of anybody else's love.

Excessive guilt, fears of abandonment or rejection, and internalized anger that is unexpressed or unacknowledged, are other psychological factors that can lead to depression. Recent research suggests that poor social skills may also predispose a person to depressive episodes.

I feel responsible for causing my own depression. Is this appropriate?

Only if you define responsibility in the most positive sense of word. That means assuming ultimate responsibility for taking care of yourself, for seeking out the best care, and for being an active participant in your treatment, not just passively receiving what's prescribed by your physician.

You are not responsible for being depressed if you define responsibility as your "fault." In psychotherapy, the goal is to understand what it means to be depressed, not to blame yourself, your parents, your boss, or anyone else. Are there things you might be doing that contribute to your depression? Sure. Should you kick yourself around the block for that? Absolutely not. It's all part of the learning process— to figure out what you may have done that contributed to your depression and how to avoid doing the same thing in the future.

As mentioned earlier, depression is an extremely complex problem. It is not reasonable or fair for you to blame yourself for a whole cascade of events—biological, psychological, and environmental—that may be contributing to your depressed state.

Chapter Four
FINDING HELP

Am I putting myself at risk if I choose not to obtain professional help for my depression?

Yes. In a worst-case scenario, you could kill yourself. You can also put yourself at emotional risk as your view of yourself, the world, and relationships gets more and more negative. If, because of your ongoing depression, your concentration is off and you stop caring, driving a car can become extremely dangerous to you and to others. By avoiding treatment, you place yourself at risk for drug or alcohol abuse in an attempt to alter or numb your feelings.

Physically, there is a demonstrated link between mental depression and overall health. Depression is associated with the blunting of the immune system, which makes depressed people more vulnerable to cold germs and other infections. One study of more than 2,400 men in Finland suggests that a pervasive sense of hopelessness is a risk factor for heart disease, cancer, and other serious medical conditions. Another study found that the risk of dying from stroke was 50 percent higher among adults with severe depressive symptoms. Susan Everson of the California Department of Health, senior author of the twenty-nine-year study, told *USA Today* that depression alters blood platelet activity in a way that could promote stroke-triggering clots.

Won't my depression eventually go away on its own if I never seek treatment?

Not necessarily. In a fairly large percentage of people, depression propagates if left untreated. Others cycle in and out of depressed moods for a good portion of their adult lives. They never learn how to deal with their depression or nip it in the bud when it returns. Untreated recurrent depressions can profoundly and even permanently affect the way you view yourself, how you relate to others, and how you deal with everyday stresses and strains.

If depression goes untreated, how long will it last?

That varies from person to person, but on average, a major depressive episode lasts a minimum of six months. As alluded to above, depression does not always go into remission spontaneously. In some cases, depression will continue indefinitely unless something is done to combat it.

I can barely drag myself out of bed. How can I be expected to motivate myself enough to see a therapist?

Everyone has an "observing ego"—the part of your psyche that can take a step back and look at things objectively, if only for a short while. To do this, you must try to separate your intellect from your emotional state. Ask yourself: "Is it reasonable for me to get help?" Even if your emotions say no, try to follow your intellect, which may be saying yes.

If you cannot use your observing ego, lean on people who love you. Ask them to read this chapter and find you a therapist. If you have no one, you can always turn to a rabbi, priest, or minister for guidance.

Why do only 20 percent of depressed people seek professional help?

Some are embarrassed because of the stigma historically associated with mental illness. For many men, depression or any mental illness signifies weakness or lack of character, so they keep quiet. Inability to pay for mental-health treatment is probably another reason many people don't seek help.

Sometimes, people don't realize they have a mood disorder because being depressed has become such a familiar feeling. Except for its length and intensity, what you feel right now may not be all that different from normal bad moods you have experienced in the past. Conscious or unconscious denial is another reason depressed people fail to get help. It's like hoping a toothache will go away and not turn into a root canal case.

How can I tell if my depression is severe enough to warrant professional help?

If, after reading the previous chapters, you are still unsure whether you meet the criteria for clinical depression, it may help to answer the following questions:

1. Do you feel an overwhelming and prolonged sense of helplessness, hopelessness, or sadness that continues no matter what you or your loved ones do to help?
2. Are you finding it difficult to perform normal activities, such as concentrating on work assignments, and your job performance is suffering as a result?
3. Do you worry all the time or expect the worst, or are you constantly irritable or on edge?

4. Are you doing things that are potentially harmful? For instance, are you drinking too much alcohol, abusing drugs, or are you overly argumentative or aggressive?

If you answer yes to any of these questions, you should strongly consider getting professional help.

Can my family doctor help me?

Perhaps. Some, but not all, primary care physicians are skilled at diagnosing and treating depression. Research has shown that all psychiatric diagnoses, including depression, are underdiagnosed and under-treated by primary care doctors, including internists, family practitioners, OB/GYNs, and pediatricians. To combat this problem, the psychiatric community has launched a major effort to train front-line doctors in how to recognize depression in their patients. Psychiatrists are encouraging primary care doctors to treat uncomplicated cases with medication, brief counseling, or both, and to refer the complicated cases to a mental health specialist. Drug companies are also trying to persuade more primary care physicians to treat depression. Antidepressants are heavily advertised in generalized medical journals, such as the *Journal of the American Medical Association*, whose readership includes many primary care doctors.

From an internist's perspective, prescribing the newer antidepressants, such as Prozac, Paxil, and Zoloft, is relatively straightforward. Doses are standardized and no blood monitoring is required, although doctors must be aware of possible adverse interactions with other drugs the patient may be taking. Unfortunately, some primary care physicians start patients with a dose that is too high or too low, and they may not be well versed in side effects, how long to continue treatment, or how to taper patients off their antidepressants.

An internist should not be expected to provide psychotherapy beyond some arm-around-the-shoulder emotional support. Internists who are comfortable treating depression ought to know when they are in over their heads. If a patient is becoming suicidal or is abusing alcohol or drugs while depressed, for example, a referral to a mental health specialist should be made.

I'm sure I was depressed during my last checkup, but my internist never asked about it. Why not?

If you consider the dizzying number of symptoms, illnesses, diagnostic tests, and medications internists need to know about, it is probably unrealistic to expect them, or any generalist, to have expertise in depressive disorders. This is unfortunate, because as many as 30 to 40 percent of people who see physicians because of medical complaints actually have a primary psychiatric disorder of depression or anxiety, which is producing real or imagined physical symptoms. Often, these patients complain of vague stomachaches or insomnia. They may tell their doctor they've lost their "edge," that they feel weak, that food doesn't taste good, or their appetite is gone. As Chapter Two pointed out, there are many subtle symptoms of depression that are easy to miss, even by a mental health specialist.

What is a mental health specialist?

A mental health specialist is a licensed professional trained in human behavior, mental health, and interpersonal relationships, as well as the diagnosis and treatment of mental illness and emotional disorders. People who specialize in mental health include psychiatrists, psychologists, clinical social workers, and psychiatric nurses. Psychiatrists are medical doctors who provide psychotherapy and can prescribe medication. Psychologists have completed a doctorate-level education or beyond and concentrate on psychotherapy. Clinical social workers generally have a master's degree in social work and are trained in various forms of counseling and psychotherapy. A psychiatric nurse is a registered nurse who has a master's degree in psychiatric nursing. These professionals usually work with psychiatrists or in psychiatric hospitals to treat people with mental disorders.

How do I know which type of practitioner to see?

Figuring out which mental health specialist to turn to can be extraordinarily difficult. The mental health system in this country is a real cottage industry; it can be disorganized, competitive, and biased. Even the most ethical mental health professional could favor a type of therapy that may not be in your best interest. On the other hand, there is a good chance that you can be helped by whichever specialist you choose.

Generally, you should let the severity of your depression determine where you go for help. Strongly consider a psychiatrist if you are suicidal or if your symptoms include manic or psychotic features (Chapter Two). Consider a psychiatrist or psychologist if there is no identifiable trigger for your depression, if you have lost or gained a significant amount of weight since your depression set in, if your symptoms have been bothering you for many months, or if you have a personal or family history of depression. A psychiatrist, psychologist, or clinical social worker can usually help where there is an obvious emotional trigger for your depression, such as divorce or financial crisis, or your depression is less severe. Psychiatric nurses usually provide counseling under the auspices of a psychiatrist.

Your attitude toward taking mood-altering drugs will also help you decide where to go for treatment. If you are unwilling to take psychotropic medication (drugs that affect the mind), you should go to a psychologist or to a psychiatrist who is willing to work within your boundaries. If you think you might need an antidepressant, a psychiatrist is—at this writing—the only mental health professional who can prescribe them in the United States.

Depending on your insurance coverage and financial situation, money can be another decision-making factor. Fees vary widely, but psychiatrists usually charge the most, up to $300 for an initial consultation and $125 to $250 for a forty-five- to fifty-minute therapy session. (Fees in major metropolitan areas are generally higher than in the Midwest and rural areas.) Psychologists charge slightly less, and clinical social workers typically charge less than psychologists. Some practitioners and mental health centers offer sliding-scale fees to qualifying patients with no insurance coverage. Some practitioners offer thirty-minute "half-sessions" or "medication sessions" for about $100 or less.

What kind of training do psychiatrists get?

Psychiatrists are medical doctors and thus have an M.D. after their name. After graduating from college, they must graduate from an accredited four-year medical school and complete four years of residency training in psychiatry. In the first year of residency, the training is in general psychiatry as well as pediatrics, internal medicine, and neurology (the brain and nervous system). Later, psychiatric residents train more thoroughly in outpatient and inpatient settings, learning about drug interventions, electroconvulsive therapy, and different modalities of psychotherapy, behavior therapy, family and marital therapy, child and adolescent therapy, and in some programs, sex therapy. Psychiatric residents also work in the emergency room doing crisis interventions, and they provide psychiatric consultations in hospital medical units, such as obstetrics and surgical wards. Like all medical doctors, psychiatrists must be licensed by the state and earn continuing education credits annually to maintain their licensure.

After completing an approved residency program, psychiatrists become eligible to apply for board certification from the American Board of Psychiatry and Neurology. Board certification, which is voluntary, is a measure of clinical competence, not excellence. The credential is earned by passing a daylong written exam that covers psychiatry and some neurology. Doctors who pass the written exam may then take oral exams. Here, the psychiatrist is observed while interviewing a psychiatric patient and then answers examiners' questions about the case. The psychiatrist also watches a video of a patient being interviewed and again answers questions. If the psychiatrist passes these oral exams, board certification is bestowed. Beyond board certification, psychiatrists can also be elected to fellowship status in the American Psychiatric Association by making a "special contribution" to the field of psychiatry.

How do I know a psychiatrist has good qualifications and training?

The "orientation"—or emphasis—of a psychiatrist's residency training program is actually more relevant than the medical school they attended. For example, psychiatric residency programs at certain hospitals emphasize psychopharmacology—treating mental illness with drugs and treating psychiatric disorders that occur in medically ill patients. Other programs stress psychotherapy. The orientation of a particular program may also change over time. At Cornell during the 1970s, for example, psychiatric residents received a superb foundation in the various forms of psychotherapy. By the 1990s, Cornell's emphasis had shifted toward psychopharmacology.

A psychiatrist in practice for twenty-five years may hold a philosophy of care that was solidified during his or her residency training. This may work to your advantage. For instance, if you are averse to taking psychotropic drugs, you may gravitate toward a doctor whose training emphasized psychotherapy. You can usually find out about a psychiatrist's residency program from the psychiatrist, from your state mental health association, or from your referring physician or hospital. Or you can consult the American Psychiatric Association's *Biographical Directory*, which contains profiles of member psychiatrists and their areas of interest or expertise.

Do all psychiatrists routinely prescribe antidepressants to depressed patients?

No. For one thing, not all depressed patients are appropriate candidates for drug treatment. Psychiatrists are trained to decide on a case-by-case basis whether drugs are needed. Some psychiatrists rarely or never prescribe antidepressants because they believe the drugs contaminate the patient's treatment. Others view antidepressants as an integral part of treatment in appropriate cases. You should feel free during your initial consultation to ask a psychiatrist about his or her prescribing philosophy.

How do I know whether a psychiatrist is keeping abreast of the latest depression treatments?

Perhaps the best indicator is an academic appointment (lecturer or assistant or associate professor) at a medical school. In many cases, these part-time clinical positions are unpaid. They usually require the psychiatrist to devote a minimum of three to five hours a week teaching medical students and residents and attending "grand rounds"—a major lecture or case conference at the hospital. This form of service and education forces the psychiatrist to remain actively involved in a profession that otherwise can be rather isolating. Another plus is being affiliated with a well-respected hospital. This provides opportunities for the psychiatrist to exchange news and ideas with colleagues.

During an initial consultation, it is perfectly legitimate for you to ask the psychiatrist about his or her hospital and medical school affiliations. Indeed, these kinds of questions indicate that you have done your homework and are likely to play an active role in your treatment.

What kind of training do psychologists receive?

After graduation from college, psychologists spend an average of seven years in graduate education training and research before receiving a doctoral degree, according to the American Psychological Association. Psychologists have either a Ph.D. or Psy.D. after their names and are trained in counseling, psychotherapy, and psychological testing. "As part of their professional training, [psychologists] must complete a supervised clinical internship in a hospital or organized health setting and at least one year of postdoctoral supervised experience before they can practice independently in any health-care arena," American Psychological Association literature states.

Like psychiatrists, psychologists must be licensed by the state or jurisdiction in which they practice. In most states, psychologists must earn continuing education credits to renew their license. Both the American Psychological Association and the American Psychiatric Association impose a code of ethics on their members. Psychologists are not medical doctors and therefore do not prescribe medication. Occasionally, psychologists work in concert with medical doctors to help patients who need both psychotherapy and medication.

Is there a turf war between psychology and psychiatry?

Yes, particularly when it comes to psychotropic medications, treatment orientation, and fiscal matters. For example, most psychologists believe that antidepressants are warranted only in certain severe cases. Psychiatrists generally believe that antidepressants can be an invaluable part of treatment for the majority of depressed patients. The battleground over the value of psychotropic drugs has a new wrinkle: at this writing, bills were pending in at least three states that would give qualified psychologists prescribing privileges.

What is a clinical social worker?

A clinical social worker diagnoses mental, behavioral, and emotional disorders in individuals, families, and groups and provides psychotherapy, according to the

National Clinical Social Work Federation. In order to practice unsupervised, the social worker must also be licensed by the state in which he or she practices. These professionals must provide a certain number of supervised psychotherapy sessions and pass an examination in order to be licensed.

Clinical social workers have either a master's or doctoral degree in social work with a concentration in psychotherapy and counseling. Clinical social workers practice in a variety of settings, including private offices, industry, schools, medical practices, mental health clinics, child welfare agencies, and community organizations.

Are mental health services generally covered by health insurance?

Most health insurance plans cover at least some mental health services, and there are efforts in Congress to force insurers to cover mental illnesses as comprehensively as they cover physical illnesses. Some insurance plans place a cap on mental health services or limit the number of therapy sessions you can have in a given year. Your written policy should tell you which mental health services are covered and to what extent. You may also ask your insurer or employee benefits coordinator which psychiatrists, psychologists, and licensed clinical social workers qualify as approved providers of mental health services under your plan.

How can I get a referral to a mental health professional?

There are a number of referral sources:

• *Your family practitioner, internist, or gynecologist.* Tell your doctor you believe you may be suffering from depression and would like a referral to a psychiatrist or psychologist who has a special interest in treating depression. If you belong to an HMO that uses a "gatekeeper" model of care, you will probably need a referral from your primary doctor in order to secure coverage for mental health services.

• *The department of psychiatry at the nearest university medical school.* The medical school or its affiliated hospital may operate a mood/affective disorder clinic. If not, solicit names of mental health professionals in your community who specialize in the treatment of depressive illnesses.

• *Your local hospital's physician-referral service.* Even if the hospital does not have a mental health program, it may be able to give you names of psychiatrists in your community. The hospital may also provide information about the psychiatrists' schooling, training, and professional affiliations. Bear in mind that hospitals refer only to psychiatrists on their own staff and don't generally refer to psychologists or social workers.

• *A private psychiatric hospital's physician-referral service or community outreach department.* Again, you will get names only of staff members, but a psychiatric hospital may be better able to refer you to someone who specializes in depression.

• *Professional associations.* The American Psychiatric Association and the American Psychological Association can refer you to their members who practice in your area. These organizations' addresses and telephone numbers appear in Appendix A.

• *Employee Assistance Programs, or EAPs.* If your workplace contracts with an EAP, you can access it directly or through your personnel or human resources department. EAPs originally were set up to help employees with substance abuse problems but are broadening their scope to provide counseling to employees with depression and certain other mental problems. EAP providers are trained in crisis intervention and can refer you to other mental health providers, if necessary. There are hundreds of EAP providers nationwide, and all are set up to protect employees' privacy. There is always a risk, however, that your supervisor or co-workers will find out or assume you are having a problem. In cases where a depressed employee's job performance is declining, supervisors may urge or require the employee to consult the EAP.

• *Community mental health centers.* These tax-supported entities charge patients on a sliding scale, according to income. Your local health department, state health department, or state department of human services can direct you to your nearest community mental health center.

• *Religiously affiliated mental health centers, such as Jewish Family Service and Catholic Family Service.* Psychotherapy at these centers is generally administered by clinical social workers, although some centers also employ psychologists and psychiatrists.

• *Clergy.* Your rabbi, priest, or minister should be able to refer you to a reputable mental health professional. Many clergy members have studied psychology and may be able to counsel you themselves. Clergy members who have a degree in pastoral counseling routinely counsel people who are depressed.

• *Friends or relatives who were successfully treated for depression.* If the therapist your friend or relative used practices too far away, that therapist may be able to refer you to a colleague who works closer to your home. Using the same therapist as your sister or mother is not always a good idea, however. In fact, some psychiatrists and psychologists avoid treating members of the same family because they find it difficult to be objective. On the other hand, some mental health professionals routinely treat several members of the same family who may or may not have a similar problem.

• *Self-help groups or patient-support groups.* Find a group near your home and attend a meeting. Chances are the members will know which therapists are best at diagnosing and treating depression. They will also know which therapists you'll want to avoid. A list of self-help groups appears in Appendix A. Another way to find these groups is through your local hospital's community outreach department.

• *Student health centers.* Most colleges and universities provide free or low-cost mental health services on campus.

• *Guidance counselor or school social worker.* If these professionals cannot help a depressed high-school student, they will know who can.

• *Magazines articles and reference books. New Jersey Monthly* is one of many regional magazines that periodically rate mental health facilities and providers in their readership area. A number of publishers put out annual health care guides that tell readers who the best doctors are in a particular geographic region, usually a large metropolitan area where there are thousands of doctors to choose from. One example is the *1997 Guide to Good Health,* published by

Philadelphia magazine. This guide includes information on mental health services and names top-rated psychiatrists in and around Philadelphia as well as southern and central New Jersey. Your public library may stock more comprehensive guides, such as *Best Doctors in America 1996–97*, by Steven Naifeh (Woodward/White). You may find the Midwest, Northeast, Pacific, Southeast, or American Central edition of this volume in your local library, or you can call (803) 648-0300 for referrals. Another resource is *How to Find the Best Doctors, Hospitals, and HMOs for You and Your Family*, by John J. Connolly (Castle Connolly Guide, 1994). A version of this paperback focusing on the New York Metropolitan area was published in 1996.

• *National Foundation for Depressive Illness* can provide a referral list of professionals in your area who treat depression. Details appear in Appendix A.

As a rule, look for a therapist who is recommended by more than one source. If you hear the same name more than once, there is a good chance that person is highly qualified.

Should I seek out someone who specializes in depression?

As mentioned in Chapter One, depression is the common cold of mental illness. So any mental health professional worth his or her salt should be able to treat most depressions, so long as the practitioner has appropriate training, experience, and credentials.

For complicated cases—depression mingled with other medical or psychiatric or personality disorders, depression caused by cancer or other medical syndromes, or in cases where somebody hasn't responded to past treatment—it makes sense to see someone who has a well-honed expertise in depression. Of course, any mental health specialist can represent themselves as being skilled in treating depression, even if they are not. Credentials are important, of course, but they do not guarantee that a psychiatrist is great at diagnosing and treating depression.

To get more substantive information, ask the therapist some of the following questions:

• *What percentage of your practice is related to depression?* Almost no one treats depressed patients exclusively. It would not be unusual, however, for a mental health professional to deal with depression in 30, 40, or even 50 percent of cases.

• *Do you teach, lecture, or write about depression?* Has the therapist ever lectured to community groups? Does he or she teach medical students and residents about depression? Has the therapist written or edited any books, chapters, or articles about depression for professional journals? Any of the above suggests cutting-edge knowledge about depression as well as a keen interest in helping depressed patients recover.

• *Were you trained specifically in areas of depression?* This goes back to the orientation of the therapist's residency or doctoral program and any subsequent training he or she may have received.

• *Are you known in the community as someone who is knowledgeable in the diagnosis and treatment of depression?* If so, the practitioner should be able to tell you how many primary care physicians routinely consult him or her when they have a depressed patient.

Until you have spent several sessions with this person, it may be impossible to know for sure whether he or she truly understands depression. Fortunately, unlike incompetence in surgery, incompetence in the mental health field is usually not life-threatening, at least not in the short run.

Ideally, you'll find a therapist who doesn't have a dogmatic agenda and doesn't view depression as *only* a sociological, physiological, or psychological phenomenon. An open mind plus training in various ways of viewing human behavior is important because depression is a multifaceted problem that often requires a multifaceted solution.

My choice of doctors is limited because I am in an HMO. How can I find the best mental health professional through my managed care network?

Very often, managed care patients must take what they can get, and the mental health specialist they are sent to may not necessarily be skilled at diagnosing or treating depression. If you belong to a large HMO, there are probably several psychiatrists and psychologists in the network. You must do some legwork to find the most appropriate one for you. If your HMO gives you names but no other information, insist on knowing more about the doctors, such as how long they have been in practice and what they specialize in. Unfortunately, that is not always an easy task if you are in the throes of depression. Your concentration skills may be lacking, and low self-esteem can prevent you from being as assertive as you need to be. If you find it difficult to persevere through the process of finding help, seek out advocates, such as family members, a family physician, or clergyperson, who can ask questions for you.

Should I go to a therapist who lives in my town?

That depends. Some psychiatrists and psychologists prefer not to treat patients who live near their home. This helps them build a powerful sense of confidentiality.

Decide how you feel about this issue. Would you feel embarrassed or uncomfortable in a chance encounter with your therapist at church, the grocery store, or party? If so, you may wish to confine your search to therapists outside your immediate area.

Is it better to work with a therapist who is the same gender as I am?

Your therapist's sex shouldn't matter. Ultimately, your therapist will seem amorphous and asexual. Sometimes, patients gravitate toward a particular therapist because of age; you may feel more comfortable with a grandmother figure, for example. Basically, you should find a therapist you feel comfortable with. There are, however, some commonsense limits to impose on yourself. For instance, an extremely seductive female patient should probably avoid a good-looking male therapist who is new to his field and lacks experience dealing with a patient's come-ons.

How do I know a particular therapist is right for me?

Assuming the therapist has proper training and adequate experience, there are three other things to look out for during your initial consultation:

1. *Is the therapist really listening and trying to understand me?* The therapist should give you his or her undivided attention. That means refusing non-emergency phone calls and barring anyone from entering the room during your session.

2. *Is this person at least as smart as me?* This is an intuitive judgment call.

3. *Is this somebody I would probably enjoy sitting next to at a cocktail party?* That doesn't mean looking for a physical attraction between you and the therapist. It means deciding whether there is comfortable communication between you to facilitate a meaningful professional relationship based on empathy and compassion.

Finding a therapist you like is almost like finding a good friend. You are looking for "chemistry," a good match between your personalities and communication styles. This assessment will be largely intuitive on your part. In general, however, look for someone who is empathic, strong, sensitive, and at least as intelligent as you are. Give credence to any negative feelings you have during your initial consultation. If, however, you have a negative reaction to four therapists in a row, the problem may lie within you.

What other personal qualities should I look for in a therapist?

Punctuality and availability are important attributes to look for in a therapist. Was he or she reasonably on time for your appointment? Is the therapist or a colleague available to you around the clock in case of emergency? Are there evening or weekend hours to accommodate your work schedule? Is the office building wheelchair accessible, if need be?

You should also ask whether treating depression is something the therapist enjoys doing. It seems counterintuitive, but many mental health professionals actually like working with depressed patients because modern treatments—both medicinal and psychotherapeutic—boast relatively high success rates. From a therapist's standpoint, helping someone move from a depressed to a happy state is enormously gratifying, professionally and personally.

Is it necessary to interview several therapists before choosing one?

Normally, prospective patients do not interview mental health providers the way that parents interview pediatricians. Your only option is to get recommendations from people you trust and have an initial consultation, for which you will be charged. It is during this first meeting that both you and the therapist will try to conclude whether you are a good match. If you do not feel entirely comfortable with the first therapist, it is perfectly appropriate to consult one or two more until you find someone you like.

What will happen during my first visit with a mental health professional?

Like all therapy sessions, this initial consultation is basically a conversation between two people where one—the therapist—is an exceptionally good listener. This session generally lasts forty-five to seventy-five minutes, during which the therapist asks enough probing questions to obtain a fair amount of information about your current problem. As time permits, the therapist also will try to understand the context of your life and how your current problem might be related to your past experiences and family history.

If you are in a crisis situation, the therapist should be able to give you feedback on the nature of your problem and suggest a treatment that can begin immediately. Otherwise, it is not unusual to end your first meeting without a clear treatment plan and without a prescription in hand. You should, however, leave feeling that you are beginning to deal with your problem and that you are in reasonably competent hands.

Although most experienced therapists can tell almost immediately whether someone is depressed, they often like to see new patients at least twice before recommending a course of action. Sometimes, a patient will act or feel differently during the second session. Seeing the same pattern of depression across at least two sessions gives the therapist a higher degree of confidence in the diagnosis. Waiting for diagnostic confidence is important because your treatment is likely to become part of your life for at least several months to come.

Chapter Five
PSYCHOTHERAPY

What is psychotherapy?

Psychotherapy, also known as talk therapy or "talking treatment," uses psychological techniques to help alleviate depression or other mental disorders. In therapy, you describe your symptoms, problems, and experiences with a therapist who, in turn, provides insightful feedback. The discussion may focus on your past or present thoughts, behaviors, emotions, and relationships. Your therapist's role is not to solve your problems, but to help you figure out your own solutions. Your therapist does this by asking carefully crafted questions and making observations designed to give you a better understanding of yourself, your relationships, and your problems. In addition, psychotherapy can help you identify negative behavioral and thinking patterns and transform them into more positive ones. The goal of psychotherapy is not only to help treat your depression, but also to improve your overall outlook on life.

Is psychotherapy the same as counseling?

Not really, although supportive psychotherapy (described later in this chapter) comes close. Instead of helping you find your own path, counseling usually presents you with a path, or a choice of paths. The emphasis is on the here and now. The counselor does at least as much or more talking than you to provide hope, guidelines, and information. Counseling can be effective for people who aren't psychologically minded, who don't want psychotherapy, or who have a specific problem they need to resolve.

While counseling places more responsibility on the counselor, psychotherapy places a greater responsibility on you to recognize negative or destructive patterns in your life and to pursue ways of breaking those patterns. As you discuss past and current feelings and experiences, the therapist serves as a conduit for your self-discovery.

Although you do most of the talking, your relationship with your therapist is deeper and more sophisticated than it would be in a counseling situation. This relationship is established through two key psychological mechanisms: 1) a therapeutic alliance, and 2) transference. A therapeutic alliance refers to the *conscious*, working relationship you and your therapist develop in order to meet common goals, such as alleviating your depressive symptoms and teaching you how to cope if those symptoms return. In transference, your *unconscious* thoughts, feelings, and reactions toward significant others are replicated with your therapist. An effective transference—be it negative or positive—is both cathartic and therapeutic. Transference may also form in counseling, and so may a therapeutic alliance, but to a lesser degree.

What are some examples of transference?

Say you had a condescending, overly critical mother. Unbeknownst to you and your therapist, your mother has been a major source of your low self-esteem and depression. In therapy, the anxiety, fear, and ambivalence you feel toward your mother flow out unconsciously and are transferred onto the therapist. Without realizing it, you are relating to the therapist in the same way you relate to your mother. This gives your therapist strong hints of how you think, feel, and react outside of your therapy sessions. Your therapist can then hold up a psychological "mirror" so you can "see" your words and behaviors more clearly, and perhaps more objectively. Ultimately, you may talk to your therapist as though he or she *were* your mother. The therapist could, in a sense, become the kind of mother you always wished you had: someone who supports your endeavors, someone with whom you can share thoughts and feelings without fear of belittlement.

Here is another example: An associate lawyer keeps getting bumped from law firm to law firm and never makes partner, even though he is very smart and good at his job. Growing up, the lawyer had a very rocky relationship with his father and learned to buck authority figures. As an adult, this attitude persisted, manifesting in the lawyer doing something or other to sabotage his relationship with each of his bosses.

In therapy, the lawyer's attitude toward authority gets replicated: He is late for appointments, or he grows hostile and nasty toward his therapist (another authority figure). Once the lawyer has transferred his feelings toward his father onto his therapist, the therapist can say, "Do you see what's happening here?" This precipitates a breakthrough in therapy. For the first time, the lawyer becomes conscious of his disdain of authority and realizes why he keeps getting fired.

Transference, even if it is not utilized so directly, is vital to your therapist's ability to help you.

How many types of psychotherapy are there?

At least seven forms of psychotherapy are in use today. Two—cognitive-behavioral therapy and inter-personal therapy—were developed with a specific focus on depression, although other forms of psychotherapy also are used to help depressed patients.

In brief, the psychotherapeutic disciplines are:

• *Classical psychoanalysis.* Developed by Sigmund Freud (1856–1939), classical psychoanalysis is the oldest and least interactive discipline. The patient lies on a couch and, through "stream of consciousness," speaks whatever thoughts come to mind. The thera-pist is out of sight, sitting behind the patient and do-ing very little talking. A great deal of time is spent looking at all the powerful components of the pa-tient's childhood and how they combined to help form his or her personality. Therapy sessions are held up to five times a week for many years. Because clas-sical psychoanalysis is designed to restructure the pa-tient's personality, and because it takes so long, Freud's method is rarely used to treat depression. Classical psychoanalysis is the treatment of choice for those who want a lengthy, detailed investigation of their personality structure and want to make sig-nificant modifications.

• *Traditional psychodynamic psychotherapy.* Like classical psychoanalysis, this modality uses early-childhood experiences, the unconscious, and trans-ference, but does so with the patient and therapist sitting face-to-face. It is thus more interactive than Freudian psychoanalysis. Traditional (versus brief) psychodynamic psychotherapy looks at personality patterns that may be related to the onset and exacerbation of depression. Severely depressed people who combine this form of psychotherapy with antidepressant medication tend to do quite well.

• *Supportive psychotherapy.* Like counseling, supportive psychotherapy focuses on the here and now. The therapist provides more guidance, advice, and direction than is available through any other psychotherapeutic treatment. The duration of therapy ranges from several weeks to several months, depending on the complexity of the patient's depression. Many social workers and psychologists provide supportive psychotherapy as well as other forms of psychotherapy. Supportive psychotherapy clearly has a place in the treatment of depression, although it has not been rigorously studied.

• *Cognitive-behavioral psychotherapy.* Originated by Aaron T. Beck at the University of Pennsylvania in the 1970s, cognitive-behavioral psychotherapy turned Freudian psychology upside down. Freud had said that how we feel influences how we think; Beck postulated that how we think influences how we feel. Inappropriately negative thoughts, or "cognitive distortions," can lead to depression, according to Beck's research. So the focus in cognitive-behavioral therapy is to explore your unconscious, your automatic thought patterns, and how those patterns affect your view of yourself, your environment, and your future. One example of distorted thinking is calling yourself a "stupid idiot" because you lost your favorite pen. Beyond thinking you are stupid, you also assume you'll always lose your pen and anything else that has importance and worth. In cognitive-therapy parlance, this kind of distorted thinking is known as an "all-or-none conclusion."

The behavioral prong of Beck's method entails the use of homework assignments. Your therapist may ask you to keep a log of how you are thinking or reacting in certain circumstances. Later, you can rewrite your cognitive distortions into more positive, more realistic language. For instance, "I'm a stupid idiot for losing my favorite pen" might be transformed into "I misplaced my favorite pen, but I'm sure it will turn up eventually."

Another log entry might describe a miserable time you had at a dinner party because Tom walked by without saying hello. You instantly assumed that Tom doesn't like you, and therefore nobody at the party likes you. In therapy, you acknowledge the possibility that Tom simply didn't see you as he made his way to the hors d'oeuvre table. You also realize that Tom's opinion has nothing to do with how others might feel toward you.

The duration of cognitive therapy is variable, lasting from several months to more than a year of weekly sessions, depending on the patient's needs.

• *Interpersonal psychotherapy (IPT).* IPT focuses on the conflicts, distortions, and difficulties that people have with their relationships with others. In session, the therapist and patient try to understand how unhealthy relationships, or unhealthy reactions within those relationships, may lead to or intensify depression. The goals of IPT are to reduce symptoms of depression, enhance your self-esteem, and improve your social functioning. IPT was developed for the treatment of depression over the last twenty years by Gerald Klerman and Myrna Weissman, and more recently by John Markowitz at Cornell University. To date, at least two research studies have shown that IPT significantly reduces symptoms in severely depressed patients.

• *Brief psychotherapy.* There are a number of different models of brief psychotherapy, but the one that has been studied most is brief psychodynamic therapy, which is a further truncated style of traditional psychodynamic psychotherapy, described above. The hallmark of all the brief therapies is specific goals. For example, the goal of brief psychodynamic psychotherapy may be to understand specifically how the past has led to depression. Brief cognitive psychotherapy might concentrate on one type of cognitive distortion and how it is feeding your depression. In brief therapy, the therapist plays a more active role, providing frequent interpretations and insights. Your past experiences, unconscious, and transference are all used, but in a more condensed form. "Brief" is a relative term. The treatment may last anywhere from a few weeks to a year. In general, short-term therapies lasting six weeks or less are insufficient for people with major depressive disorder. People with milder depressions can probably benefit from a course of treatment lasting sixteen weeks or less, however.

• *Pluralistic psychotherapy.* This approach folds certain aspects of various psychotherapeutic techniques into one treatment. For example, your therapist might focus on your relationships, your cognitive distortions, and your childhood at different points during your treatment. A pluralistic approach can become sloppy if the therapist is not well-versed in all the modalities. Pluralistic psychotherapy can be effective if a depressed patient doesn't respond to a single form of talk therapy.

Which forms of psychotherapy are considered best for depression?

Cognitive-behavioral and interpersonal psychotherapy are the only clinically proven treatments for all forms of depression, including major depression and dysthymia. Studies of brief psychodynamic psychotherapy have yielded mixed results. The other forms of psychotherapy are clearly effective for many depressed people, but rigorous investigations are still being conducted.

If I say, "I hate myself," what might my therapist's response be, using some of the different psychotherapeutic methods?

In psychoanalysis, your therapist would probably ask, "When have you felt that way before?" and "How does it make you feel now?"

In cognitive-behavioral therapy, the response could be, "What are you thinking that makes you conclude that you hate yourself?"

In interpersonal therapy, your therapist might say, "What goes on in your relationships with other people that makes you hate yourself?"

Wouldn't it be better for my therapist to simply point out that I have many good qualities and that I shouldn't hate myself?

Naturally, a primary goal in psychotherapy is for depressed patients to recognize and embrace their positive, admirable qualities. However, it is rarely helpful for a therapist to simply point out those qualities. Doing this could make the therapist appear too wise, which risks further diminishing a depressed patient's self-image. The impact of treatment is far more powerful and long-lasting when your therapist helps you do your own psychological work in order to discover and acknowledge your positive attributes.

How will my therapist decide what kind of psychotherapy to use with me?

Since most therapists are trained in several psychotherapeutic disciplines, the choice depends largely on your individual needs and the therapist's expertise and beliefs. If you are accustomed to a logical way of thinking and are more comfortable with your intellect than your emotions, your therapist may recommend cognitive therapy because it's didactic and won't threaten you on an emotional level. If, on the other hand, you are very interested in how you relate to others, interpersonal psychotherapy may work best. If one type of psychotherapy proves ineffectual after the first several sessions, your therapist may switch to another type or try a pluralistic approach.

Following are three composite sketches of patients who received appropriate forms of psychotherapy:

Brief psychodynamic therapy: Carol, a forty-two-year-old homemaker, notices an insidious onset of the blues. Over the next two months, she loses interest in her volunteer work at the local hospital, grows less concerned about her appearance, and has trouble falling asleep. When her symptoms worsen, she makes an appointment with a psychotherapist. During her first session, Carol is asked if anything in her life has changed recently. She mentions that her daughter, Tina, recently left for college. Carol expresses surprise at how much she misses Tina. She also expresses a tremendous sense of loss and even anger because Tina "abandoned" her. Those emotions make Carol feel guilty because she wants her daughter to be happy and independent.

When her therapist asks Carol if she had ever experienced this particular set of feelings before, she relates that her mother had died when she was a freshman in college many years ago. Over the next few therapy sessions, Carol is able to grieve and mourn the loss of her mother and express her anger—at both her mother and daughter—without feeling guilty. Later, Carol comes to realize that Tina's going off to college triggered a painful, domino effect of emotions surrounding her mother's death— emotions that were never worked out in the past. Toward the end of her treatment, Carol is able to tease through the multiple layers of her losses. After six months, she feels better and is able to end therapy.

Cognitive-behavioral therapy: Bill, a fifty-five-year-old executive, has just been laid off after twenty years with the same company. Soon afterward, he begins to experience stomach pain, constipation, insomnia, and a greatly diminished appetite. Fearing he has bowel cancer, he sees his family doctor. Bill undergoes a series of tests, but all the results are negative. His insightful practitioner points out that Bill's job loss has placed him under considerable stress and urges him to see a cognitive-behavioral therapist. In therapy, the central theme of Bill's life becomes clear: his self-worth has always been attached to his external achievements. In high school, he was captain of the baseball team, and he thought that was the only reason he got a date for the prom. In college, Bill got into the fraternity he wanted because, he believed, his prowess in mathematics enabled him to do the accounting for his fraternity house. After entering the business world, he worked extremely hard and was rewarded financially—until his company downsized. Throughout his life, Bill was never able to feel his worth internally. So when he lost his job, Bill felt diminished as an employee, a father, a spouse, an uncle, and a human being. In therapy, Bill learns to recognize how distorted his thinking has always been. He also learns that his feelings about himself have an enormous impact on his mood in general. After several months of therapy, he grows out of his depression and begins to look at life in a more positive way.

Interpersonal psychotherapy: Dorothy, a sixty-eight-year-old retired teacher, and her husband, Alan, move from Boston to an exclusive retirement village in Arizona. Dorothy had been looking forward to the sunny weather, but despite the pool, golf course, and beautiful climate, she feels uncomfortable and irritable in her new surroundings. She has no desire to decorate her new house. She begins waking up early and having crying spells. Dorothy can't seem to remember phone numbers of friends she left behind. At Alan's urging, Dorothy makes an appointment with a psychotherapist. As Dorothy and her therapist examine her interpersonal relationships, they notice a lifelong pattern of her extreme dependence on other people. To Dorothy, relationships have always equaled safety. When she moved, she left a wide circle of friends, family members, shopkeepers, and others who made her feel safe and needed. Without really knowing it, she was very dependent on these people in an unhealthy way, and she couldn't function well without them. Her interpersonal psychotherapy focused on helping Dorothy develop a more balanced view of her relationships. She came to see that moving to Arizona presented a rare opportunity to form healthier relationships with new friends as well as with her husband. Over the year she remained in therapy, Dorothy's depression lifted, and she was able to be more mature and less dependent in her relationships.

Is it important for me to know which kind of psychotherapy my therapist will be using?

Only if you are interested. Some people want information about the psychotherapeutic process; others do not. If asked, psychotherapists should offer research data and other information explaining why a particular form of psychotherapy is indicated.

Elizabeth, age fifty-one, was so fascinated by the process of psychotherapy that she continued weekly sessions long after her major depressive episode had ended in the mid-1970s. "Now that I had rescued my faltering marriage and was functioning normally," she recalls, "I looked back to see where I had been, the depths to which I had fallen, and how I had managed to climb out. And I was curious about the process. I realized that I had a very unique opportunity, with a therapist who knew me really well, to think through some other areas of my life, such as a bad relationship with my mother that I didn't understand. I thought that maybe this kind of therapy could be proactive rather than reactive. The question wasn't 'Can I get even better?' but 'Can I get to be my best?'"

Using a combination of classical psychoanalysis and cognitive therapy, Elizabeth sorted out pieces of her childhood and previous behaviors and realized that her depression probably had a genetic component: both her mother and grandmother had displayed depressive symptoms. Elizabeth learned how to avoid stressors that could possibly trigger another depressive episode. Eighteen months after her depression had lifted, Elizabeth ended therapy, only to return about a year later when her father became seriously ill "and all the family crazies started happening."

It was during this second eighteen-month therapy stint that Elizabeth "found and understood ways of accessing all of my strengths, all of my assets, and all of my potential." Furthermore, she adds, "I focused myself enough to see me as others saw me—and to solidify my decision to pursue a career I had always wanted."

What percentage of patients with major depression respond to psychotherapy?

Research has shown that unless psychotherapy patients are also taking antidepressants, the majority will not get significantly better. When psychotherapy is combined with antidepressants, the vast majority of patients improve.

Various studies over the last fifteen years have found that, overall, treatment for major depression is effective in 65 to 85 percent of cases. Some mental health specialists believe those figures are low; in their experience, up to 98 percent of severely depressed patients get significantly better when psychotherapy is combined with antidepressants.

Is group therapy helpful in the treatment of depression?

As a solo therapy, group therapy probably has fairly low efficacy, although this modality has not been rigorously studied. Professionally led group therapy (Chapter Seven) can, however, be beneficial when coupled with individual psychotherapy, medication, or both. Peer-led support groups and twelve-step programs can also be useful adjuncts to psychotherapy.

Which form of psychotherapy works best for people with bipolar disorder?

Psychotherapies for bipolar disorder have not been as rigorously studied as psychotherapies for depression. Because bipolar disorder is clearly a physiological condition, and since many manic-depressives live very chaotic lives, psychotherapy often takes a more supportive focus.

Usually, the first goal is to stabilize these patients on medication. Once the patient is stabilized, the psychotherapy should be tailored to the individual's personality. In most cases, the psychotherapy is brief and focused, centering on helping patients clarify their judgments and gain insights into their behaviors and their disorder.

How long does a psychotherapy session last?

In almost all cases, a psychotherapy session runs forty-five to fifty minutes. With the exception of classical psychoanalysis, sessions normally take place once a week. Your sessions may be scheduled twice a week in the beginning if you are unable to function or there are concerns about your safety.

What if I develop a crush on my therapist?

You should bring it up in therapy and talk it through. Therapists are trained to deal with these situations and to hide any discomfort they might feel. Therapists are further trained not to take advantage of patients' vulnerability. If your therapist returns your affections, either verbally or physically, it is a serious breach of professional ethics. By becoming romantically involved with a patient, the therapist risks losing his or her license to practice—and you risk emotional devastation.

If talking with your therapist about your attraction fails to water down your feelings, it makes sense to consult another therapist. The consulting therapist should be able to tell you whether to make a change or to continue therapy and wait for your romantic feelings to dissipate.

The development of strong emotional reactions, including sexual ones, toward your therapist can occur regardless of your therapist's age, appearance, or gender. Some patients want to become their therapist's "best friend." Less common is falling in love with your therapist, a phenomenon known as "erotic transference." In reality, erotic transference is a form of "resistance"—building an unconscious (not willful) emotional barrier to the therapeutic process. By the same token, if you never develop any strong feelings toward your therapist, it could mean that healthy transference is not developing.

Is it ever appropriate to hug my therapist?

Probably not. The psychotherapeutic environment is a safe haven, and a hug can have very different meanings at different times, depending on how you are feeling toward your therapist at the moment. If you are having an erotic transference, you might misconstrue a hug as a come-on. If you are having a negative transference, a hug might make you feel uncomfortable. Of course, therapists try to maintain a sense of humanity. They may shake your hand hello and good-bye and give you a tissue if you are crying.

But in general, it is inappropriate and unprofessional for a therapist to hug, kiss, or otherwise touch a patient, aside from shaking hands. The therapist's goal should be to help you feel huggable to the rest of the world.

If I need antidepressants, will I be required to also undergo psychotherapy?

Not necessarily, although your doctor will want to see you every few months to check on your dosage, side effects, and response to the medication. Research has shown that, for severe depression, antidepressants coupled with psychotherapy is only slightly more effective than antidepressants alone. Accordingly, many psychiatrists will comply if a patient wants antidepressants without psychotherapy. And some psychiatrists simply don't believe in giving medication without at least some psychotherapy.

Shouldn't my therapist attempt psychotherapy first, and if insufficient progress is made, suggest an antidepressant?

That depends on how profoundly depression has affected your life. If you have all the severe markers of depression and are suicidal, your therapist should not say, "Let's talk for a few months and see what happens," and risk having you kill yourself. If you are not suicidal but are dripping with depressive symptoms—frequent crying spells, significant weight loss, insomnia, agitation—you should probably be encouraged to begin antidepressant treatment right away. People with "softer" depressions—those who can function relatively well despite their symptoms—and patients who are very opposed to taking psychotropic drugs and are not suicidal, should not be pressured to go on medication.

Can antidepressants ever interfere with psychotherapy?

No, although this is one of the greatest concerns expressed by depressed patients. In fact, the converse is true. When your antidepressant kicks in, you'll get more energy, your concentration will improve, and you'll see your life from a more balanced perspective. Those three factors alone will result in a higher yield from the psychotherapeutic experience. When you are not feeling so crushed by depressive symptoms, your observing ego—that intellectual part of your psyche—can step forward in therapy with more aplomb.

Will I look forward to my therapy sessions, or will I dread them?

That will depend largely on how you feel about the notion of psychotherapy. In the beginning, some people breathe an enormous sigh of relief as they walk into their therapist's office; others are filled with trepidation or anxiety. As the course of therapy evolves, the nature of your relationship with the therapist, as well as the nature of your transference, will dictate whether you look forward to your sessions. Be aware that your feelings about therapy and your therapist will probably change from session to session. This is normal. Some days, you may not be in the mood for having your psyche probed. Other days, you'll look forward to venting pent-up frustrations in the safe environment of your therapist's office. If you *always* look forward to therapy—or *always* dread it—there is probably something wrong.

How am I supposed to feel after a therapy session?

You will most likely experience a wide range of feelings after your sessions. Depending on your mood and what happened during therapy, you may feel less depressed, more depressed, enlightened, provoked, annoyed, energized, or emotionally drained. Psychotherapy is not designed to be an easy process. You will be rolling up your "emotional sleeves" and working very, very hard to understand yourself better and to conquer your depression. Even if a session is particularly difficult, you should still walk away feeling that the encounter had value. At the end of each session, you should feel that the therapeutic alliance continues to exist between you and your therapist, and that your connection with your therapist is a positive one. These feelings are central to a healthy psychotherapeutic experience.

I cannot fathom spilling out my problems to a therapist whose life is probably so much better than mine. How can I overcome these feelings of powerlessness and jealousy?

It may help to focus on your areas of expertise: Your therapist is an expert on understanding human behavior; you are an expert on yourself, even if you don't yet realize it. You are embarking on a therapeutic journey with a person whose life's work is devoted to helping people just like you.

Resenting or envying your therapist because his or her life is allegedly better than yours can make the journey take longer. Just because your therapist seems mentally healthy now, he or she may have had depression or another emotional problem in the past. We are all human and therefore all potentially vulnerable.

I am a very private person. What if I wish to keep certain feelings or experiences to myself?

It probably won't affect your treatment outcome. Simply state up front that there are certain issues you do not want to discuss in therapy. Your therapist should be willing to respect your boundaries. Lying to hide a secret or to test your therapist's perceptions is probably not in your best interest. Therapists are not mind readers, and they are not quite as perceptive as people assume they are. If you want to deceive or trick your therapist, you can.

Remember that psychotherapy is a collaboration. It is perfectly appropriate to hold certain secrets close to your heart. Your therapist does not need to know everything about your life in order to help you. Nonetheless, at the end of an early session, many therapists routinely ask, "Is there anything you want to tell me that might be embarrassing or upsetting that you should probably tell me anyway?" Asking such a question doesn't necessarily mean you will disclose information, but it does give you permission to do so. By asking this question, your therapist is sending you a signal that he or she has the strength and nonjudgmental attitude to tolerate whatever you might say. The embarrassing slice of life you wish to get off your chest may very well fit into a pattern the therapist is seeing in you. But if your deep, dark secret is that you beat up Billy Smith in the third grade, it may have nothing to do with your current mood disorder.

In a sense, you and your therapist will paint a canvas together. You need not fill in each and every cloud or ray of sunshine, but both of you must be able to recognize what's in the painting.

Is it good to let myself cry during therapy?

Yes. But if you want to cry for forty-five minutes straight, you can do it much less expensively at home.

How many sessions will I have to go through before I start feeling better?

That depends on how severely depressed you are, how motivated you are to get well, whether you are taking an antidepressant, and how skilled your therapist is. If your depression is mild or moderate, and you have no history of depression, you may begin to feel better after three or four sessions, even if you are not taking antidepressants. If you are taking medication, it may take up to four to six weeks before you notice your symptoms beginning to subside. If you have major depression, and you are not taking medication, you may never feel significantly better with psychotherapy alone, research has shown. This can be a very frustrating experience for both you and your therapist. Many severely depressed patients find that antidepressants take the "edge" off their dark mood, enabling them to see their lives more clearly and objectively and progress more rapidly in psychotherapy.

Do health insurance plans normally cover psychotherapy?

Coverage depends on the type of plan you have and your diagnosis. Many plans limit the number of mental health visits you can have in a year, and life-time caps on mental health treatment are not un-usual. As a result, many patients pay for their treatment out of pocket.

I've heard that therapists recommend many more sessions than are needed just so they can make more money. How can I prevent this from happening to me?

A certain percentage of mental health practitioners take psychotherapy beyond its reasonable limits. There are several possible reasons for this, including:

1. They are not trained well enough to know how and when to end therapy;
2. They are greedy;
3. They made a very strong attachment to their patient and cannot let go; or
4. The clinical situation is very complicated.

To prevent your sessions from continuing end-lessly, you should always be willing to say, "Where are we in therapy?" or "Is it time to stop?" All forms of psychotherapy have a beginning, middle, and end. If your therapist cannot give you a clear indication of where you are and how far you have to go, it is probably a bad sign. At this point, you may wish to consult with another therapist to get an outside evaluation of your progress.

Sometimes, patients develop a resistance during the course of psychotherapy; they'll want to drop out of treatment prematurely because a therapist they previously liked now seems offensive. If this happens to you, try to evaluate your treatment based on all your sessions, not on a single disconcerting remark or session. Figuring out the appropriate time to end therapy is much more art than science.

Should I expect a smooth course of recovery, or will there be setbacks before I get healthy again?

The latter is more likely to be true. Human emotion, behavior, and experience cannot be plotted on a perfectly smooth curve. The same goes for psychotherapy, where many of your feelings, behaviors, and experiences get replicated. Occasional setbacks are part of the process.

It may help to think of depression as a frozen pond, and recovery from depression as the melting process. Ponds don't melt uniformly; they crack in places, refreeze in others, and turn into slush. But inevitably, when springtime comes, all the ice is gone.

Can psychotherapy backfire?

Yes. Usually it happens because the psychotherapist is either incompetent or uses an inappropriate form of psychotherapy, or the patient is overtly or covertly self-destructive.

Take, for example, a man in a severe depressive episode, which is primarily physiological, and he has an enormous amount of suppressed aggression. He also tends to rationalize—he concocts elaborate but untruthful explanations to hide the genuine motivations behind his actions, thoughts, and feelings. Each time he rationalizes in session, his therapist points out what he is doing and suggests that his rationalizations are preventing him from getting to the heart of his depression. The patient, who has a tremendous fear of losing control, grows visibly uncomfortable and anxious each time the therapist attacks his deep-

PSYCHOTHERAPY   107

seated self-defense mechanism. Finally, in a fit of anger and frustration, the patient quits therapy and feels worse than he did when he began.

An astute therapist should know when someone's self-protective mechanisms are best left alone. Antidepressants coupled with a less probing, more intellectual approach, such as cognitive-behavioral psychotherapy, probably would have been more effective in this patient's case.

How can I be sure my therapist will maintain my confidentiality?

It is unlikely that a therapist will have a position of respect in any community if he or she does not maintain patient confidentiality. The issue of confidentiality is taught and ingrained from day one of any therapeutic training program, be it psychiatry, psychology, or social work. If confidentiality is not maintained, people and colleagues know that, and the therapist won't get referrals.

The only time a therapist must, by law, breach confidentiality is when a patient is imminently suicidal. Here, the therapist has the legal, ethical, and moral responsibility to intervene. The therapist might give the patient a choice of going to the hospital voluntarily, having the therapist petition the court for an involuntary commitment, or setting up a system whereby a significant other keeps tabs on the patient. Some therapists have had to call the police or rescue squad to take a suicidal patient to the hospital.

How do therapists keep track of all their patients?

New therapists and therapists in training typically take copious notes of psychotherapy sessions; they may even tape-record them, with the patient's permission. But after a while, therapists learn to remember what goes on in session in the same way they would recall an hour-long conversation with a friend. To do their jobs well, therapists must be active listeners; they need to concentrate on what you are expressing in order to give you meaningful feedback. A few key words jotted into your chart after each session is generally enough to jog an experienced therapist's memory—even if you are one of a dozen depressed patients the therapist saw that week. Memorizing what goes on in therapy becomes as automatic as driving a car.

Chapter Six
ANTIDEPRESSANTS

What is an antidepressant?

An antidepressant is a prescription drug designed to remove depressive symptoms by changing the function and structure of brain tissue. Despite what you may have heard or assumed, antidepressants are not "happy pills," and they do not make you "high." In fact, mentally healthy people who take antidepressants feel no difference in their mood. In people who are clinically depressed, antidepressants uplift the mood directly and indirectly by blocking the negative aspects of depression. Feelings of low self-esteem and worthlessness, appetite loss, lack of interest, insomnia, and virtually all the symptoms of depression slowly evaporate. In addition, the medication helps restore the patient's energy level and powers of concentration.

How were antidepressants discovered?

Like many scientific breakthroughs, the first antidepressant was discovered serendipitously. In 1952, iproniazid, a derivative of an antibiotic used to manage tubercular infections, was given to patients with tuberculosis (TB). The drug did not work particularly well against TB, but doctors noticed a compelling side effect: the TB patients who took iproniazid enjoyed a prolonged elevation in their mood. Imipramine, the second drug found to produce antidepressant effects, was introduced in 1957. Subsequent antidepressants were developed based on chemical structures of the known antidepressants.

How many antidepressants are there?

More than two dozen antidepressants are approved for use in the United States, and more are always under development. The most frequently prescribed antidepressants fall into one of six drug classes, or families: monoamine oxidase inhibitors (MAOI), the oldest class; tricyclic antidepressants (TCA); selective serotonin reuptake inhibitors (SSRI), the newest class; tetracyclic antidepressants; "novel or heterocyclic" antidepressants; and stimulants.

Following is a list of the major antidepressants in each category. Drugs are identified by their generic names followed by their brand names:

Monoamine Oxidase Inhibitors
phenelzine (Nardil)
tranylcypromine (Parnate)

Tricyclic Antidepressants
amitriptyline (Elavil, Endep, Enovil)
clomipramine (Anafranil)
desipramine (Norpramin, Pertofrane)
doxepin (Adapin, Sinequan)
imipramine (Tofranil)
nortriptyline (Aventyl, Pamelor)
protriptyline (Vivactil)
trimipramine (Surmontil)

Selective Serotonin Reuptake Inhibitors
fluoxetine (Prozac)
fluvoxamine (Luvox)
paroxetine (Paxil)

sertraline (Zoloft)

Tetracyclic Antidepressants
amoxapine (Asendin)
maprotiline (Ludiomil)

Novel or Heterocyclic Antidepressants
bupripion (Wellbutrin)
mirtazapine (Remeron)
nefazodone (Serzone)
trazodone (Desyrel)
venlafaxine (Effexor)

Stimulants/Amphetamines
methylphenidate (Ritalin)
dextroamphetamine (Dexedrine)
pemoline (Cylert)

There is yet another family of drugs, the mood stabilizers, that are occasionally prescribed for depression. These include lithium (Cibalith-S, Lithane, and others), valproic acid (Depakote), and carbamazepine (Tegretol, Epitol).

Why do antidepressants have such strange-sounding names?

Drugs are named and classified according to the mechanism by which they act on the brain, or to describe their molecular structure. Monoamine oxidase inhibitors, for example, inhibit monoamine oxidase—the enzyme that breaks down norepinephrine. This results in more norepinephrine being made available in the brain. Similarly, selective serotonin reuptake inhibitors increase the availability of serotonin.

If you examine the molecules of the tricyclic antidepressants, you will see a three-ringed structure.

Tetracyclic molecules have four rings, and hetero-cyclics have variable numbers of rings.

How do antidepressants work?

As with many medications, antidepressants' exact mechanisms of action are not fully understood. It is clear, however, that antidepressants normalize the brain's mood centers. As you may recall from Chapter Three, the mood centers are a collection of brain cells, or neurons, that spread out through the brain. Neurons communicate with one another through chemicals called neurotransmitters, including serotonin and dopamine. These neurotransmitters are called "first messengers" because they hook up with receptors on the outside of neurons. This leads to a cascade of intercellular events known as the "second messenger system," which somehow triggers DNA to make other changes in the cells that control mood.

In depression, there may be too much or too little neurotransmitter, the communication between the first and second messenger systems may be incomplete, there may be an abnormality in the receptors on the cell's surface or interior, or a neurotransmitter may be functioning inefficiently. Antidepressants influence, at least indirectly, the neurotransmitters, receptors, and activity inside neurons that control mood. SSRIs, for example, selectively block the absorption, or "reuptake," of serotonin in the area of the receptor. Instead of serotonin getting sucked up by the cell and pulled out of the way, an SSRI makes more serotonin available to the myriad of serotonin receptors on brain cells. So, theoretically, more serotonin attaches to more receptors, thus creating a greater capacity for the receptors to facilitate communication inside the mood centers.

Why are there so many different drugs for depression?

Depression is a devastating disorder that afflicts 1 out of every 10 people in the United States and untold millions around the world. The level of human suffering and economic loss has researchers at universities, medical schools, and pharmaceutical companies working fervently to develop better and better depression treatments.

In addition to the urgency of preventing suicide among depressed individuals, there is a huge economic incentive to discover more effective drugs to treat depression. Not surprisingly, antidepressants represent a multibillion-dollar-a-year industry. Patients normally take antidepressants daily for a minimum of six months; some remain on medication for the rest of their lives. With the majority of depressed people currently untreated, the potential to relieve suffering—and to increase profits—through awareness campaigns is astronomical.

How will my doctor decide which antidepressant is right for me?

In recent years, the SSRIs—Paxil, Prozac, and Zoloft—have emerged as the first line of treatment for most depressions. This has occurred because, on balance, SSRIs seem to be the safest and most effective antidepressants on the market. SSRI side effects tend to be much less cumbersome than those associated with many of the older antidepressants, especially the tricyclics. And unlike MAOIs, SSRIs do not require a restrictive diet.

Despite all that, psychiatrists do not automatically prescribe Prozac or one of its cousins to every depressed patient who walks through the door. The type, severity, and longevity of your depressive symptoms all help determine your treatment. For instance, withdrawn patients are often given one of the more stimulating antidepressants, such as Wellbutrin or Vivactil. People with agitated depressions and prominent insomnia tend to get sedating antidepressants, such as Desyrel, Ludiomil, or Serzone.

Why has Prozac gotten so much more media attention than the other antidepressants?

Discovered in Europe in 1974, Prozac was the first SSRI to reach the United States. Since its FDA approval in the late 1980s, Prozac has earned a reputation of being a very, very effective antidepressant that works on a great many serotonin receptors in the brain. Its impact on brain chemistry is so far-reaching that it became the first drug used for three psychiatric diagnoses: depression, obsessive-compulsive disorder, and panic disorder. It is no surprise, then, that Prozac initially was seen as a "magic bullet" that Americans always seem to be searching for.

Unfortunately, the early excitement over Prozac led to a lot of misinformation, spread by the media and by word of mouth. A huge public controversy over the drug ensued. In the early 1990s, the book *Listening to Prozac* by Peter D. Kramer asserted that Prozac not only treated depression but also modified personality. Soon afterward, *Talking Back to Prozac* by Peter R. and Ginger Ross Breggin reviewed Prozac's potential downsides, including sexual dysfunction and anxiety. Then came *Beyond Prozac* by Michael J. Norden, which focused on natural depression antidotes and prevention. These books fueled the raging debate over the risks and benefits of Prozac and other antidepressants. All the controversy made Prozac a widely discussed drug in the 1990s, just as Xanax grabbed headlines in the 1980s, and Valium became a media darling in the 1970s. Next year, some other psychotropic drug will likely get all the attention.

In reality, Prozac is probably no better or worse than the other SSRIs. SSRIs are safer for the heart than some other classes of antidepressants, but SSRIs can cause headaches, tremors, agitation, nervousness, and insomnia, as well as sexual dysfunction in both men and women. SSRIs do not, however, trigger panic attacks when taken as directed. And recent literature shows they do not alter your personality. It can seem that way, though, if you have been suffering from dysthymia (chronic depression), low-grade panic disorder, or social phobias for a long time. People who did not know you before your disorder set in may see you as a "new person." In actuality, you are getting back to your normal self. By taking Prozac or any antidepressant, you are modifying an underlying, diagnosable psychiatric disorder—not reshaping your soul.

I know someone who was given Xanax for depression. Is this drug effective?

When Xanax (alprazolam)—a member of the Valium family—was introduced in the United States in 1981, it was touted as the first anti-anxiety drug that also had antidepressant properties. But studies revealed inconsistent results. Xanax is an anti-anxiety medication sometimes prescribed to relieve anxiety and panic disorder. Incredibly addictive, Xanax has also become a major drug of abuse in this country.

How long must I take antidepressants before I begin to feel better?

The time it takes for an antidepressant to work ranges from one to six weeks, with an average of two to four weeks. However, up to 35 percent of people who take antidepressants experience an immediate positive placebo effect because they expect the medication to work. Positive side effects also may emerge soon after starting drug therapy. For example, a sedating antidepressant may begin to relieve insomnia after the first or second dose. A good night's sleep gives you more energy during the day.

Why don't antidepressants alleviate depressive symptoms faster?

Antidepressants work on a long, slow, complex cascade of events involved in intercellular communication in the brain. Also, antidepressants are administered in small but increasing dosages until a therapeutic level of the drug is reached in the bloodstream. The slow-acting nature of all antidepressants, and the urgency at which severely depressed patients need relief, has researchers looking for new antidepressants that act more quickly.

What does it feel like to be on an antidepressant?

In time, you will probably feel like your old self again, which may give you a dramatic sense of relief. Any elation you feel will stem from the disappearance of your depressive symptoms, not from the drug itself. You may not even realize the benefits of your treatment until much later, when you examine your mood in retrospect.

While antidepressants are highly effective at removing depressive symptoms, they obviously will not solve all your problems. They simply put you on the road to figuring out your own solutions.

What percentage of patients who take antidepressants get better?

Statistically, 65 to 85 percent of depressed people who take antidepressants get better. However, there are many, many psychiatrists and psychopharmacologists (experts in medications used in psychiatric disorders) who believe the actual success rate exceeds 95 percent. It may take a lot of trial and error before the right drug, or combination of drugs, at the correct dosage is determined for you. But when that happens, there is an extremely good chance that your depressive symptoms will go away.

Should people with major depression always be offered an antidepressant?

With so many relatively safe and effective antidepressants available today, people with major depression certainly have a right to this form of treatment. But medication should never be forced on anyone. Some people are very opposed to psychotropic drugs and prefer to talk things through. Psychotherapy alone is usually worth a try and can sometimes relieve depression or at least help people get through a depressive episode. But statistically, the most effective treatment for major depression is a combination of antidepressants and psychotherapy.

Why is that?

There are at least three reasons psychotherapy and antidepressant modalities work so synergistically:

1. Psychotherapy supports you emotionally until your antidepressant takes effect, or until the right antidepressant is found;
2. Antidepressants help you regain the clarity and strength you'll need in psychotherapy to understand yourself and the sources of your depression better; and
3. Weekly psychotherapy has a built-in monitoring system for your medication's efficacy and side effects.

Which symptoms usually respond to antidepressants first?

There is no clear pattern, although many patients report that insomnia is the first symptom their antidepressant begins to attack. You may also notice a very, very subtle shift in your mood initially. Within the first week or so, you may feel a little less negative, a little less hopeless and sad, or you may have a little less difficulty getting out of bed and making it through the day. As time goes on, your ability to concentrate may begin to improve. You may have less and less trouble falling asleep, and you'll stop waking up hours before your alarm clock rings. You may develop an appetite for something, or start reading the newspaper again. There is no way to predict which symptoms will go away first, or in which order.

What is the typical dosage schedule for antidepressants?

With three notable exceptions, most antidepressants are normally taken once a day. This dose schedule could very well change as newer versions of these drugs emerge. For example, Wellbutrin, historically taken twice a day, now comes in a sustained-release preparation and may be taken less frequently.

When should I take my medication?

Whether you take your pill in the morning or at night often depends on whether the medication has a stimulating or sedating side effect. If the drug is sedating, it is best to take it with a snack a half hour before bedtime. Some antidepressants, including the SSRIs, have a stimulating effect when you begin treatment and become more sedating over time. In these cases, patients should change the time of day they take their pill. Most antidepressants must be taken with food to prevent gastrointestinal distress. If possible, take your first dose at a time of day when your doctor is easily accessible in case you have a bad reaction.

Are there many adverse side effects associated with antidepressants?

Yes. A large number of adverse side effects have been reported by antidepressant users over the years, and the vast majority of people who take antidepressants experience adverse side effects to one degree or another. The good news is that some adverse side effects subside over time. Others can be controlled by manipulating the dose or time of day you take your antidepressant, or by adding another medication to your drug regimen.

The most prominent side effects caused by the tricyclics include dry mouth, constipation, difficulty urinating, postural hypotension (dizziness upon standing up abruptly owing to a drop in blood pressure), heart palpitations, blurred vision, sweating, stimulation or sedation, weight gain, and, occasionally, sexual difficulty.

MAOIs typically cause significant postural hypotension, difficulty with orgasm, sedation and insomnia, dry mouth, weight gain, and, more rarely, stimulation. MAOIs can also provoke a "hypertensive crisis"—if you eat the wrong food or take the wrong drug when you are on an MAOI, your blood pressure can rise so rapidly and dramatically that it may cause a stroke. Classic symptoms of stroke are a headache in the back of the head, along with sweats and nausea. MAOI users should be given an antidote to keep with them at all times that will take down their blood pressure, just in case.

In addition to sexual dysfunction and anxiety, other SSRI side effects may include gastrointestinal upset (often in the form of heartburn or diarrhea), dizziness that is unrelated to blood pressure, lightheadedness, and a dull headache.

Most of the novel or heterocyclic and tetracyclic antidepressants share similar side effects with both the tricyclics and SSRIs. The most common of these side effects are stimulation or sedation, stomach upset, light-headedness, and headaches. People on MAOIs or tricyclics often feel more "drugged" than people who take SSRIs or novel or heterocyclic antidepressants.

A list of possible side effects will accompany your prescription. Provided by your pharmacy, these lists are comprehensive and may include side effects that are frightening but extraordinarily rare. Discuss any concerns you might have with your doctor.

How much weight will I gain if I take a drug with this side effect?

Weight gain varies widely among patients, ranging from several pounds to many pounds. Weight gain may have something to do with tricyclics' slowing down the metabolism slightly, or antidepressants' general tendency to increase carbohydrate cravings. You may prevent weight gain by being more vigilant about your diet while taking your antidepressant. Also, as your depression lifts, you will have more energy to exercise regularly.

Antidepressants not associated with as much weight gain include Wellbutrin and Serzone.

What kind of sexual problems can be caused by antidepressants?

Inability to achieve orgasm, reduced or loss of sexual desire, difficulty becoming aroused during sex, inability of the penis to become or stay rigid, premature or nonexistent ejaculation, and reduced semen output all have been reported by users of antidepressant medications. Some antidepressants are more notorious than others for certain forms of sexual dysfunction. For example, MAOIs tend to block orgasm, while SSRIs slow down ejaculation and repress sexual drive. In fact, almost everyone who takes an SSRI will experience these or other sexual side effects. Two antidepressants with minimal or no sexual side effects are Wellbutrin and Serzone.

I have no interest in sex now. If I take an SSRI or MAOI, how will I know if sexual dysfunction is being caused by the drug or by my depression?

Before you begin taking antidepressants, inform your doctor of any past or current sexual problems. It may be possible to find a medication or dosage level that minimizes certain sexual side effects. At the very least, knowing your sexual history will help your doctor determine later on whether a sexual symptom is connected with the medication. Also, it is possible that your interest in sex will return after your depression lifts.

Is there anything I can do to alleviate the sexual side effects of my medication?

There are a variety of ways to combat your medication's sexual side effects. For instance, your doctor may allow you to take a "drug holiday" by skipping your medication on Friday and Saturday if you are planning a special weekend. A different strategy is to take your antidepressant as scheduled but add another drug, such as Periactin, before you go to bed. Periactin is a serotonin antagonist; it blocks the effects of serotonin, which the antidepressant presumably is making more available to brain cells. Periactin should not be used too frequently, because it will interfere with the antidepressant's beneficial effects. Also, Periactin is sedating. If you are not planning to fall asleep after making love, you may wish to try Ritalin, a stimulant, to enhance your sex drive. Because of its addiction potential, Ritalin should be used only as a last resort. Another drug your doctor may suggest is Yocon, which was originally used for male impotence. Yocon, a general sexual stimulant, does not interact with antidepressants but can make people nervous. Ginkgo biloba, a fruit-bearing tree native to China, is being investigated as a treatment for sexual side effects.

Don't be shy about discussing your sexual symptoms, side effects, or concerns with your therapist, even if the therapist neglects to ask about them. Open communication with your significant other is equally important. Unless your partner understands that your sexual symptoms are drug induced or part of your depressive illness, he or she may erroneously assume something is wrong in your relationship.

What can I do to lessen some of the non-sexual side effects of my antidepressants?

Here are some things you can try:

• To relieve constipation, drink eight glasses of water a day, increase your intake of live acidophilus cultures (found in yogurt and acidophilus milk), and consume foods high in soluble fiber. If you use a Metamucil-type laxative, do not take it with your medication, because the fiber will block absorption.

• To relieve dry mouth, drink lots of water, suck sugar-free hard candy, or eat frozen green grapes. Dry mouth may also respond to one of the over-the-counter preparations, such as Saliva Substitute. If all else fails, your doctor may recommend Salogen, a prescription drug designed to increase saliva flow.

• If your antidepressant makes you dizzy when you stand up quickly, simply stand up more slowly. You may also want to increase your salt intake if your blood pressure is low in general.

• The dull headaches associated with SSRIs are treatable with any of the nonprescription analgesics.

• You can compensate for blurred vision by holding reading material at a slightly greater distance from your face than usual. Be extra careful when driving a car. If you will be taking your antidepressant for a long period of time, wearing glasses or changing your eyeglass prescription may help. Blurred vision, far more common with the tricyclics than any other class of antidepressants, tends to scare patients because they think there is something wrong with their eyes. But the medication affects the muscles behind the eyes, not the eyes themselves.

Knowing what to expect before you begin drug treatment will help you plan your coping strategies. Your doctor should explain which side effects to anticipate. For example, knowing in advance about postural hypotension could mean the difference between falling as you rise from a chair and preventing injury because you deliberately stood up slowly.

Will I experience side effects before the drug begins to work on my depression?

Yes; most people feel worse before they begin to feel better. This is another reason doctors normally prescribe a low dose and work up to a therapeutic dose over the course of several weeks. Try not to let the adverse effects discourage you. Let the fact that your body is being affected by the medication give you hope that you will soon enjoy a positive response.

Given all the adverse side effects, why would anyone want to take antidepressants in the first place?

The consequences of not treating depression are potentially more serious than side effects. As a result, many patients perceive adverse effects as mere annoyances, not deterrents to treatment. Nevertheless, you and your physician should carefully analyze the "risk/benefit ratio" before you decide whether to take an antidepressant. In some cases, the risk of adverse effects is not worth the potential gain. So, if you have a mild depression and drive a truck or work with power tools for a living, it may not be prudent to take an antidepressant. If you are a mildly or moderately depressed schoolteacher, and psychotherapy hasn't helped, the potential benefits of taking an antidepressant probably outweigh the risks. If you are debilitated by your depression, side effects are no big deal if the antidepressant can help you reclaim your life.

Do adverse side effects worsen or lessen over time?

Again, there is no predictable pattern to the severity or duration of antidepressant side effects. Some will go away on their own, others will not.

Can antidepressants affect my fertility or ability to carry a pregnancy to term?

There is no consistent or reliable research assessing the fertility rate among antidepressant users, although antidepressants can theoretically affect the menstrual cycle. There are no significant data suggesting antidepressants appreciably increase the risk of miscarriage.

Is it safe to take antidepressants during pregnancy?

The little research that has been done to answer this question has yielded somewhat mixed results. One study out of the University of California–San Diego looked at several hundred women who had taken Prozac during pregnancy. No increase in the risk of miscarriage or major birth defects was found. Taking Prozac in the third trimester did, however, increase the newborn's risk for low birth weight, breathing difficulties, and other minor problems, according to the study. A more recent study by Toronto researchers found that prenatal exposure to Prozac or a tricyclic antidepressant made no difference in a young child's IQ, behavior, temperament, or language skills. Although these two small studies—published in the *New England Journal of Medicine* in October 1996 and January 1997, respectively—offer reason for optimism, their findings have yet to be replicated by larger studies. And there are no controlled studies examining the long-term effects of prenatal exposure to antidepressants, although preliminary data look reassuring.

Unless her depression is life-threatening, a pregnant woman should probably try psychotherapy and other drug-free remedies first. If she is still depressed, she should avoid antidepressants during the first trimester, if possible. After that, she should weigh the unknown risks to her baby against the known risks that depressive symptoms place on a pregnancy. For example, a severely depressed woman who doesn't take her vitamins or get proper prenatal care is putting her baby's health at risk. Depression that continues after the baby is born can interfere with mother-infant bonding.

Will I harm my baby if I take antidepressants while breast-feeding?

All antidepressants leach into breast milk, but it is unknown whether this hurts the baby or whether the baby will experience withdrawal symptoms after weaning. Most psychiatrists recommend against breast-feeding while on antidepressants. Infant formula may be less ideal than breast milk, but a depressed mother cannot nurture her baby as well as she could if her depression were adequately treated.

What are the chances that the first antidepressant my psychiatrist prescribes will work?

Research has shown that between 50 and 60 percent of patients respond to initial antidepressant treatment. Of those who don't, the vast majority get better after switching medications.

What will happen if I have to switch antidepressants?

That depends on the medications involved. If you are switching from one of the MAOIs (Nardil or Parnate), you must wait at least two weeks before starting treatment with another antidepressant. If you are switching *to* an MAOI from Prozac, you must wait five weeks (two weeks if you were taking one of the other SSRIs). Otherwise, too much serotonin can build up in your system. This can cause a life-threatening stroke, or a condition known as "serotonin syndrome." Symptoms of serotonin syndrome include restlessness, tremors, muscle spasms, and confusion. In Chapter Nine, you will find a variety of ways to cope with your depression until your new medication begins to work.

Just because your first antidepressant isn't doing much to alleviate your depressive symptoms, that doesn't necessarily mean you have to switch medications. Sometimes, taking a second antidepressant will kick-start your medication into action. Your doctor may try adding a small amount of a tricyclic to an SSRI regimen, for example. Or you might try augmenting your treatment with an entirely different drug, such as lithium, Cytomel (the thyroid hormone T3), BuSpar (a non-addictive anti-anxiety drug), Parlodel (an anti-Parkinson's drug), Tindal (used to treat a variety of emotional disorders), or Visken (a beta-blocker normally used to treat high blood pressure or migraines). Stimulants, such as Ritalin, are also sometimes used to augment treatment.

You should not consider augmentation until your antidepressant has had sufficient time to work on its own—four to six weeks. If you do augment, you may or may not need to take the additional medication throughout your full course of treatment.

Would any diseases or medical conditions rule me out as a candidate for antidepressants?

In people with untreated bipolar disorder, antidepressants can shift their depression to mania. If you have hypertension, probably the only antidepressant to avoid is Effexor, which may raise blood pressure. If you have low blood pressure, you should avoid tricyclics and MAOIs, both of which can decrease blood pressure. You should also be wary of the tricyclics if you have hyperthyroidism, heart problems (such as mitral valve prolapse), or any systemic disease that increases the heart rate. People with irritable bowel syndrome should probably avoid SSRIs, because they can cause diarrhea. Certain antidepressants and dose levels are potentially harmful to patients with heart, liver, or kidney disease.

Are there any medications I should avoid while taking antidepressants?

It is dangerous to take certain antihistamines, such as Seldane, while on an SSRI. Anticholinergic and sympathomimetic medications (used in certain allergy and cold remedies, as well as in anesthesia, some gastrointestinal medications, and certain ophthalmologic drugs) may aggravate the side effects of some of the tricyclic antidepressants. Do not worry, however, if you need emergency surgery while taking an antidepressant. Chances are there will be no significant adverse drug interaction. Surgeons and anesthesiologists are well-trained to monitor patients for drug interactions.

Will I have to take any tests prior to starting antidepressant treatment?

Yes. The same battery of blood tests used to rule out medical causes of depression also help determine antidepressant treatment (Chapter Two). These include the "chem screen," complete blood count (CBC), thyroid profile, and electrocardiogram (EKG). In addition, there should be a urinalysis to check for normal kidney function, because antidepressants are often excreted through the kidneys.

How often will I see my doctor while I am taking an antidepressant?

Usually, patients need one or two appointments to establish a diagnosis before getting a prescription. If you are to have psychotherapy, your practitioner can monitor your response to the medication during your regular sessions. Otherwise, you will probably be asked to come in or call after two to four weeks of antidepressant treatment to report how you are feeling and whether you are having any adverse side effects. Naturally, if you have a severe or unexpected reaction, you should notify your doctor immediately. Once you are stabilized on medication—which can take anywhere from two weeks to three months— your doctor will probably want to monitor your blood pressure and side effects and observe and discuss your clinical response about once a month.

Will I need blood tests while on antidepressants?

It depends on which drug you are taking. Some antidepressants, such as Pamelor, have a "therapeutic window"; the drug won't work if you are taking too little or too much. A blood test is the best way to determine if you are taking an appropriate dose. Anyone on tricyclic antidepressants should undergo periodic blood tests to make sure the correct amount of medicine is in the blood, since too much can become toxic.

Researchers have recently identified certain markers in the blood that signal a problem in long-term Prozac users. It seems that everyone who takes Prozac, or other SSRIs, for an extended period of time (months for some, years for others) gets tired. This places them at risk of falling asleep at the wheel. SSRI-induced fatigue is associated with the buildup of a certain metabolite (by-product of the drug being broken down by the body) in the blood. If this happens, the patient is often taken off medication for several weeks to allow the metabolite to wash out of the blood before resuming treatment. Patients, particularly Prozac users, who follow this new strategy usually get their energy back. Depression usually remains in remission, because SSRIs have a long-lasting effect in the brain.

Patients taking other antidepressants potentially would benefit from periodic blood monitoring, but tests do not yet exist for all of them. Ultimately, doctors hope to have blood tests for every antidepressant on the market.

How much do antidepressants cost?

Depending on where you live, which pharmacy you use, and sometimes your dosage, antidepressants average about $1.60 to $2 a day. That translates to $48 to $60 a month, or $584 to $730 for a twelve-month course of treatment. Some drug companies vary prices according to dosage; others charge the same regardless of dose.

My health plan doesn't cover prescription drugs. Is there any way of cutting my costs?

Yes. Ask your psychiatrist for free samples left by drug company representatives. If paying for your medication is a hardship, your doctor may be able to give you up to several months' worth of samples. Another way to save money is through the drug companies themselves. Most drug companies have mechanisms to provide a limited amount of antidepressants free to patients who could not otherwise afford them. Ask your doctor how you can take advantage of these programs.

Using generics also can lower your costs. Many antidepressants, including all the tricyclics, come in these less expensive versions. Unfortunately, generic antidepressants have a wide range of variability, so their potency and bioavailability are less predictable than the name brands'.

Is it better to discontinue taking an antidepressant after my depression has gone away, or to stay on medication indefinitely?

For a first episode of major depression, you should continue taking antidepressants for a minimum of four to six months *after* experiencing a "full therapeutic response," meaning your depressive symptoms have gone into remission. Remember, it takes four to six weeks on average for a full therapeutic response to occur.

There are no hard-and-fast guidelines for patients who have had two episodes of major depression that were not life-threatening. If you have had three or more major depressive episodes, or one or two life-threatening episodes, you should probably continue on antidepressants indefinitely. This guideline is based on a study out of the University of Pittsburgh, which found that 80 percent of patients with recurrent depression who remained on medication stayed depression-free. By contrast, only 20 percent of those who went off medication at any time stayed depression-free.

In the past, American psychiatrists generally thought recurrent depressions could be prevented with a half-dose antidepressant. They now realize that a half-dose isn't enough. The dose that removes your depressive symptoms will be the same as your so-called maintenance dose.

Even if you meet the criteria for open-ended antidepressant therapy, you still have a right to try going off medication to see if your symptoms return. Do not, however, stop taking your pills without your doctor's supervision.

Can long-term antidepressant therapy be harmful to my health?

Tricyclics can theoretically cause some cardiac difficulty, including heart block, a condition in which the passage of impulses through the heart's conducting system gets interrupted. This can lead to dizziness, fainting, or strokes. Oddly enough, tricyclics also have antiarrhythmic properties, which means they can prevent irregular heart rhythms. The rule of thumb is to stay away from tricyclics if you have cardiac disease.

Can antidepressants cause cancer?

There are no hard or consistent data showing that any of the antidepressants cause or exacerbate cancer. In fact, antidepressants are frequently prescribed to depressed cancer patients.

Has anyone ever died from taking an antidepressant?

Yes. Death by antidepressants is exceedingly rare, but it can happen in several ways. You could suffer a fatal allergic reaction called anaphylactic shock. In almost fifty years of antidepressant use worldwide, only a handful of these cases have been reported. If your medication is improperly prescribed and inadequately monitored, you can have a sudden cardiac arrest. Also, a willful overdose can result in death. Tricyclics' effect on the cardiovascular system makes them particularly dangerous. If taken all at once, a one- or two-week supply can produce serious, potentially fatal cardiac complications. In fact, tricyclic antidepressants are now the leading cause of death by drug overdose in the United States. It is a cruel irony that medications so effective in combating suicidal depressions have such potential lethality. Fortunately, the newer antidepressants (for example, the SSRIs) are safer in an overdose situation.

Can antidepressants affect my dreams?

Yes. All antidepressants, except Serzone, affect sleep architecture, including REM (rapid eye movement) sleep—the stage of regular dreaming—and stage IV sleep, the time when frightening dreams and nightmares can occur. Patients, especially those taking SSRIs, typically experience an increase in dreams, probably because they spend a little less time in REM sleep and slightly more time in stage IV. Although sleep patterns during antidepressant treatment aren't as pure as normal sleep patterns, they beat the insomnia so often associated with depression.

After going off your medication, your REM-stage dreams may temporarily increase in intensity and frequency. This phenomenon is known as "REM rebound."

How should antidepressants be taken?

While each patient's treatment plan is individualized, some generalizations can be made. As mentioned earlier, your medication will likely be started at a low dose to make sure you can tolerate it and to give your body a chance to get used to the drug's effects. If you are in good health, the dose will be increased every two to seven days, as tolerated, until it reaches its therapeutic range. For the elderly or infirm, the interval between dosage increases is lengthened, generally to seven to fourteen days. Also, the total dose for elderly people is usually lower because their bodies tend to be more sensitive to the medication.

Are allergies to antidepressants common?

Less than five percent of patients will develop a rash, usually within twenty-one days of starting medication. As mentioned above, a very tiny percentage of the population—far less than one percent—has a severe or life-threatening allergic reaction.

If I develop a rash from taking one kind of antidepressant, should I avoid other antidepressants in the same family?

Not necessarily. Rashes are caused by a drug's chemical structure, not its function. If you are allergic to the SSRI Paxil, for example, you certainly wouldn't want to take Prozac, another SSRI, because the drugs are so similar chemically. But you could probably take Zoloft, another SSRI, because it has a different chemical structure.

Which medications are best for bipolar disorder?

While lithium remains the standard-bearer in the treatment of bipolar disorder (manic depression), many psychiatrists are now turning first to valproic acid (Depakote), and carbamazepine (Tegretol, Epitol)—anticonvulsants used for years in the treatment of epilepsy. While none of these drugs is great at blocking depressive symptoms, they are extremely effective in blocking the recurrence of depression, and they can also block mania. Other medications for bipolar disorder include the angina medication verapamil (Calan) and clonazepam (Klonopin), a central nervous system depressant. Two new anticonvulsants—gabapentin (Neurontin) and lamotrigine (Lamictal)—are also being prescribed to treat bipolar disorder.

Are there any foods I should avoid while on antidepressants?

The only antidepressants with dietary restrictions are the MAOIs (Nardil, Parnate). Probably the most dangerous foods to MAOI users are sauerkraut and marmite (a green vegetable jelly from Britain). Other foods and beverages to be avoided include beer, red wine, aged or smoked cheese, brewer's yeast, liver, pâté, soy sauce, fava beans; herring, sausage, and other smoked or pickled meat, fish and poultry; and many types of Chinese food. All these substances are high in the amino acid tyramine. If you are taking an MAOI, you are blocking an enzyme that usually breaks down tyramine. By eating the aforementioned foods, a tyramine buildup can occur, dangerously raising blood pressure.

Can I safely drink alcohol or smoke marijuana while on antidepressants?

Probably not. While imbibing during antidepressant therapy is not necessarily dangerous, research suggests it can undermine the effectiveness of your medication, especially during the first few months of treatment. Also, alcohol itself is a depressant and may therefore aggravate your symptoms. For these reasons, psychiatrists advise patients to abstain, or at least to keep alcohol consumption to a bare minimum, while on antidepressant medication.

Marijuana is also probably best avoided. Marijuana's active ingredient, THC, is a hallucinogen and probably acts on the same neurotransmitters being manipulated by antidepressants. Also, THC is fat soluble, so it lingers in the brain for a long time. For similar reasons, cocaine and other illicit drugs should be avoided, as well.

Can antidepressants make someone commit suicide?

Not directly. The greatest risk of suicide ironically occurs during that window of time when people begin to regain energy but are still depressed because their antidepressant has not yet reached a therapeutic level in the bloodstream for a long enough time. Once their energy returns, some depressed patients find the willpower to kill themselves.

Several years ago, there was a controversial study that found Prozac increased a person's risk for suicide. When the research was systematically reviewed, however, the data were found to be flawed; there was no evidence that Prozac led to or caused suicide. Yet there is a very, very rare phenomenon where patients report feeling suicidal when taking antidepressants when they did not feel suicidal before. Experts are not sure what to make of these reports. It may be a pharmacological effect, or a psychodynamic effect. Perhaps it stems from an inappropriate sense of failure or shame for having to resort to medication.

Both patient and mental health professional must be vigilant regarding the patient's feelings about suicide. These feelings can often be dispelled through good psychotherapy combined with a strong support network of family and friends.

Will my antidepressant's effectiveness wear off over time?

A small minority of patients will build up a tolerance for their antidepressant and require a larger dose. In a few cases, antidepressants stop working entirely. The reasons for these phenomena are only beginning to be investigated.

Can depressed children safely take antidepressants?

Yes, but their antidepressant should be prescribed by a competent child psychiatrist who has training in psychopharmacology.

Are antidepressants addictive or habit-forming?

Not physiologically, although people can become psychologically dependent on antidepressants. Interestingly, patients who protest going on antidepressants in the beginning are often the most skittish about coming off them later on. They feel so good that they are afraid their depression will return.

Will I have withdrawal symptoms when I stop taking my antidepressants?

Probably not if you are weaned off your medication slowly. If you stop taking your antidepressant cold turkey, your withdrawal symptoms will vary according to which drug you were on. Tricyclic antidepressant withdrawal symptoms may include nausea, vomiting, and drooling. Abrupt cessation of SSRIs can produce a transient "head rush," or sense of electricity in the head. The other antidepressants also can cause some minor discomfort, including headaches and malaise, when you stop taking them. Fortunately, withdrawal symptoms are not dangerous.

Coming off antidepressants gradually has other possible advantages: it may reduce the risk for a recurring depression or even normalize your brain chemistry permanently.

What would happen if I stopped taking my medication prematurely?

Depressive symptoms could rebound. Research indicates that if you stop taking antidepressants before four months, there is an 80 percent chance that your depression will come back.

What should I do if I don't respond to any antidepressant protocol?

A good first step is to consult with one or two psychopharmacologists, who can review your case very carefully and determine whether there is another drug or drug regimen that might help. Many psychiatrists have expertise in psychopharmacology. If yours does not, obtain a referral from your psychiatrist, local hospital, medical school, or directory of mental health professionals in your local library. Or you can contact the American Society of Clinical Psychopharmacology (see Appendix A).

If all else fails, there are still many other treatments you can try. You will learn about them in the next chapter.

Chapter Seven

OTHER THERAPIES

Aside from psychotherapy and medication, how many treatments are available to help depressed people?

While the majority can be helped through psychotherapy, antidepressants, or both, there are several other treatment options—ranging from the orthodox to the unorthodox. Hospitalization, electroconvulsive therapy ("shock treatments"), light therapy, acupuncture, exercise, and meditation all may relieve or prevent depression to varying degrees. St. John's wort and other herbal remedies are gaining popularity even though questions about their safety are, as yet, unanswered. There is also a new, experimental treatment called repetitive transcranial magnetic stimulation (rTMS), which has demonstrated some benefit in the treatment of major depression, but much more research needs to be done.

HOSPITALIZATION

When is hospitalization for depression necessary?

Hospitalization is sometimes necessary for severely depressed patients after all attempts at outpatient treatment have failed. Hospitalization is also warranted when someone is imminently suicidal, homicidal, or has been neglecting their health to the point where their life is in danger. People may also be hospitalized when their pharmacological treatment is very complex and needs close monitoring, or if they are suffering from serious medical problems in addition to depression.

The decision to hospitalize someone is never made lightly; hospital treatments for severe depression are sometimes available on an outpatient basis, particularly when the patient has a strong support network of family and friends. Outpatient treatment is also known as "partial" or "day" hospitalization, in which a patient is in the hospital from nine A.M. to five P.M. and goes home each night. If inpatient treatment is required, the psychiatrist should give the patient a chance to go to the hospital voluntarily. If the patient refuses, and the psychiatrist believes the patient is dangerous to himself or others, the psychiatrist is obligated to seek a court order for an involuntary hospital commitment.

Inpatient treatment for depression can take place in a public or private psychiatric hospital, or in the psychiatric unit of a general hospital. There, a team of mental health specialists often use an intense, multidisciplinary approach to help depressed patients recover.

What will happen to me in the hospital?

Treatment protocols vary from hospital to hospital; some psychiatric facilities are more medically oriented, while others are more psychotherapeutically or psychoanalytically oriented. But in general, there are a number of standard procedures all patients go through. Initially, you will be examined by an internist, family doctor, or psychiatrist whose goal is to identify any medical problems. A psychologist will administer psychological tests designed to analyze personality patterns and to detect organic illnesses that might affect personality. You will sleep in a private or semiprivate room and eat with other patients in a dining room. Patients wear street clothes, not hospital gowns. Staff also dress in street clothes.

Each day will include a number of different types of psychotherapy. These may include individual therapy, group psychotherapy, vocational therapy, and recreational therapies, such as athletics, art therapy, and movement or dance therapy. Family therapy may be added if significant family discord or marital difficulties exist. Here, your spouse, parents, or children learn about the nature of depression, how to cope with your disorder, and how to assist in your recovery. Family therapy is also offered to healthy families.

Most sessions take place three to five times a week. The psychiatrist who admitted you may or may not be involved in your individual therapy and probably won't be involved in your other therapy sessions. Staff psychiatrists, psychiatric residents (under supervision by staff psychiatrists and chief residents), clinical social workers, or recreational therapists will conduct your other sessions. If you are to receive electroconvulsive therapy, your psychotherapy schedule will be modified to support you and orient you if you are confused after treatment.

In addition, you will be exposed to "milieu therapy"—the notion that the psychiatric unit can itself be therapeutic. Patients are free to share their thoughts and feelings with one another, and to console and encourage their fellow patients. These exchanges typically occur at mealtime, leisure time, in group therapy sessions, and in other group settings. In some psychiatric facilities, patients hold community meetings to discuss hospital politics, aesthetics, and services. These meetings give patients a sense of empowerment.

Even if you choose not to communicate with other patients, the mere presence of other people will remind you that you are not alone.

Are depressed patients grouped together in the hospital?

Not usually. Psychiatric units are often filled with psychiatric patients with a variety of diagnoses, such as panic disorder, schizophrenia, and depression. Patients also come from a broad spectrum of socioeconomic backgrounds. The philosophy for this is that a psychiatric facility ought to reflect the real world as much as possible. In recent years, however, many teaching hospitals have created specialized units for mood disorders, or have begun grouping patients with depression or manic depression in a separate unit.

What is group therapy?

Group therapy usually includes six to ten patients and one or two psychiatrists, psychologists, or social workers who serve as leaders. Each session may have a theme, such as the impact of depression on relationships or the shame of depression, or there might be no theme—just an open-ended discussion. Patients are encouraged to do most of the talking, with the leaders acting as catalysts to move the discussion forward. Through this process, therapeutic forces are created. Group therapy aims to help patients change problem behaviors and teach them how to cope with their illness.

What is a recreational therapist?

According to the *1991 Dictionary of Occupational Titles*, a recreational therapist, also known as a therapeutic recreation worker, plans, organizes, and directs medically approved recreation programs for patients in hospitals and other institutions. Among other things, these therapists direct and organize sports, dramatics, games, and arts and crafts to help patients develop interpersonal relationships, to socialize more effectively, and to develop confidence needed to participate in group activities.

What is vocational therapy?

Vocational therapy helps patients identify their aptitudes and interests and plan their return to work or school. As you may recall from Chapter Two or know from personal experience, depression can wreak havoc on your professional or scholastic life, as well as your personal relationships. Vocational therapists can, for example, help patients get ready for job interviews and teach them how to budget expenses and plan meals if they are to live alone after leaving the hospital.

How long is the average hospital stay for depression?

Currently, the average length of stay is about two weeks. As is true of all forms of hospitalization, the length of stay in psychiatric hospitals has decreased dramatically over the last fifteen years. Primarily, this has been a function of third-party payment and managed care. Better treatment has also been a factor. For people hospitalized for depression, limitations on length of stay can create problems, however, as some treatments take longer than two weeks to work.

How much does it cost to be in a psychiatric facility?

That varies widely from hospital to hospital, but it is not unheard of for some places to charge $1,000 a day. Check with your health insurer to find out how many hospital days will be covered.

Are private psychiatric hospitals better than public hospitals for treating depression?

No. Whether a hospital receives public funds has little to do with the quality of care it provides. More telling is whether it is affiliated with a good medical school, and the experience and board certifications of the people who work there.

Every so often, various magazines publish stories ranking the best hospitals in the United States. In 1996, *U.S. News & World Report* ranked Massachusetts General Hospital in Boston, C. F. Menninger Memorial Hospital (Topeka, Kansas), McLean Hospital (Belmont, Massachusetts), Johns Hopkins Hospital (Baltimore), Columbia-Presbyterian Medical Center (New York), Mayo Clinic (Rochester, Minnesota), and New York Hospital–Cornell Medical Center (New York) as among the best hospitals for psychiatric care. The hospitals were ranked according to their reputations among leading psychiatrists.

My psychiatrist thinks I should check into a psychiatric hospital, but I'm embarrassed and afraid. What should I do?

Embarrassment, fear, and related emotions are natural, appropriate, and they ought to be discussed openly with your psychiatrist and loved ones. Hopefully the benefits of being hospitalized will far outweigh the trepidation you are experiencing. If you are concerned about what others might think, remember that you have the power to keep your situation confidential. Your hospitalization is no one else's business but your own, your psychiatrist's, and your immediate family's.

ELECTROCONVULSIVE THERAPY

What is electroconvulsive therapy?

Pejoratively known as "shock treatments," electro-convulsive therapy (ECT) involves passing a brief electrical current through the patient's head via electrodes placed on one or both sides of the scalp. This produces a brief generalized seizure, or convulsion. The convulsion alters the brain's chemistry in a way that often relieves symptoms of depression or other emotional and mental disorders, albeit temporarily. Some studies have shown that ECT alters the same neurotransmitters that are affected by antidepressants. There is further evidence that ECT also stimulates the endorphin system. Endorphins are hormones that act as natural opiates, which lift the mood.

How can an electrical charge change the chemicals in the brain?

Despite thousands of studies of ECT, scientists still do not fully understand how this happens. The only aspect of ECT that seems to consistently correlate with the alleviation of depressive symptoms is having a convulsion. A convulsion is the electrically induced repetitive firing of the neurons in the brain. This rapid firing of nerve cells somehow modifies the chemical messenger systems. A good analogy is cardio-conversion, a procedure that electrically shocks the heart to restore a normal rhythm. However, ECT utilizes far less electricity. High-tech ECT equipment enables the doctor to precisely control the amount of electricity passing through the brain.

How long does the seizure last?

A few seconds. The body remains motionless during this time, because the patient is first sedated and then given a light general anesthetic plus a medication to temporarily paralyze the muscles. The seizure is detected by changes in brain wave patterns that are displayed on an EEG (electroencephalogram) machine. Another way to detect the seizure is by watching for very subtle neurological signs such as the fanning of the toes (Babinski's reflex) or goose bumps on the skin.

Under what circumstances is ECT used for depression?

In most cases, ECT is a treatment of last resort for severely depressed people who did not respond to repeated attempts at antidepressants and psychotherapy. ECT is also offered to patients who need relatively rapid relief from a severe depressive episode because they are suicidal or debilitated by their condition. Depressed patients with delusions or severe "vegetative symptoms," such as lack of interest, low energy, and melancholia, may also be candidates for ECT. Depressed elderly patients may be given ECT if antidepressants are considered dangerous to their health.

Is electroconvulsive therapy given to everyone who is hospitalized for severe depression?

While some people are hospitalized for the express purpose of receiving ECT, no depressed hospital patient receives this treatment automatically. In fact, the majority of people in the hospital for depression do not receive ECT. Whether ECT is used depends on the patient's particular needs plus the philosophies of the admitting psychiatrist and the hospital. ECT can also be administered on an outpatient basis.

How many ECT sessions are needed?

A typical course consists of six to ten treatments, although some patients need more. ECT is generally administered two to three times a week, with at least one day between treatments. Patients often feel less depressed after the first or second treatment session. But then a peculiar thing happens—many patients begin to feel worse toward the middle of their treatment course. By the end of treatment, however, almost all patients begin to feel better again. If too few treatments are administered, the beneficial effects will be very transient.

Who is with the patient during an ECT treatment?

Usually a team consisting of a psychiatrist, an anesthesiologist, and a psychiatric nurse work together to administer ECT.

How effective is ECT?

Studies have shown that ECT helps 80 to 90 percent of depressed patients. This compares favorably with antidepressant treatment, which is effective in 65 to 85 percent of cases. As with other treatments for depression, the benefits of ECT may wear off after several months. A relapse can sometimes be prevented by taking antidepressants for about six months following ECT, although patients who didn't respond to medication prior to ECT often won't benefit from the drugs afterward. Another strategy to prevent relapse is to administer a short series of maintenance ECT periodically, usually on an outpatient basis. Maintenance ECT can be given to block the signs and symptoms of depression before they occur, or it can be administered at the first signal that depression is returning. Of course, some patients respond to their first course of ECT and never have a relapse.

If ECT is more effective than antidepressants, why isn't it used as a first line of treatment for depression?

Aside from its stigma, which turns off many patients, the treatment is much more disruptive to a person's lifestyle compared to taking a pill once or twice a day or seeing a therapist once a week. Even as outpatients, most people cannot work during their course of ECT treatment because they are too groggy or confused. ECT is also considerably more expensive than antidepressants and psychotherapy.

How much does ECT cost?

The cost of a single ECT treatment generally ranges from $650 to $1,000. This covers use of the ECT room (usually a surgical facility), ECT equipment, medication, the anesthesiologist's fee, and the psychiatrist's fee. In most cases, ECT is covered by health insurance.

Does ECT cause memory loss?

Yes, especially when the electrical charge is delivered through two electrodes on the scalp rather than one. In fact, memory disturbance is the most troubling side effect of ECT, but fortunately it is usually temporary. Memory loss and confusion begin as soon as patients regain consciousness, around thirty minutes after treatment. They may have difficulty remembering addresses, dates, names, and phone numbers. In addition, memories of many events that occurred in the weeks leading up to and following ECT are difficult or impossible to recall. Memories of the ECT treatment itself are also lost. Memories usually return after several days or weeks, although mild memory loss may continue for many months, and some patients have reported memory problems years after treatment. A tiny percentage of people have permanent difficulty learning new information and recalling old information after bilateral ECT. Unilateral ECT—delivering electricity to the brain through an electrode placed on one side of the scalp—is associated with far less memory loss but may require a couple of extra treatments.

The potential for memory loss discourages many depressed people from trying ECT, although some patients change their mind after being educated about the procedure. Information about ECT may be provided by your psychiatrist as well as the hospital where ECT is administered. If your doctor hasn't answered all your questions, ask to speak to someone who is an expert in ECT technology as well as its physical and emotional impact on patients.

Aside from memory loss, are there other side effects associated with ECT?

Patients usually wake up from ECT with a dry mouth and a headache. There is a small risk of cardiac difficulty during ECT, but hospitals are equipped to deal with such emergencies.

Are there any contraindications for ECT?

Brain lesions, such as a tumor that increases pressure in the brain, and cardiovascular disease often rule out people for ECT. However, there are no absolute contraindications.

Can ECT cause brain damage?

Anatomically, there appears to be no damage caused by ECT. What, if any, damage occurs at the cellular level or neurotransmitter level in the areas of memory and learning is not so clear. Research is ongoing into ECT's long-term effects on the brain.

If ECT is so effective for depression, why does it remain so controversial?

The potential for memory loss is the only understandable, rational reason for ECT's tainted reputation. For the most part, all the other reasons for avoiding ECT stem from a lack of appropriate education and unfair biases. It is hard to forget the horrific scenes from Ken Kesey's classic *One Flew Over the Cuckoo's Nest*, where ECT helped support Kesey's metaphorical tale of an oppressive society. ECT has never been used to punish or control patients, and modern ECT methods protect patients from thrashing about during the seizure. Despite its shortcomings, ECT has saved many lives.

My psychiatrist thinks I could benefit from ECT, but the whole idea seems scary. What should I do?

Unless there is an urgent, life-or-death need for ECT, you are wise to weigh all the risks and benefits before deciding whether to undergo treatment. By reading this section, you have taken an important first step—you have begun to inform yourself about ECT. Another important step is discussing your feelings with your loved ones or your psychiatrist. Or you can seek a second opinion. It may also help to talk to a person who has undergone ECT. One of the self-help groups listed in the back of this book may be able to put you in touch with someone who has had ECT. Former patients' perceptions vary widely, according to a 1985 National Institutes of Health Consensus Development Conference Statement on ECT. Some patients perceive the procedure as a terrifying experience or an "abusive invasion of personal autonomy," the consensus panel found. Some patients felt shame because of the social stigma they associate with ECT, and some reported "extreme distress from persistent memory deficits." The panel also heard "moving testimony from former patients who regarded ECT as a wholly beneficial and lifesaving experience."

REPETITIVE TRANSCRANIAL MAGNETIC STIMULATION

What is repetitive transcranial magnetic stimulation?

Repetitive transcranial magnetic stimulation (rTMS) is an experimental, ECT-like procedure in which a handheld coil generates a magnetic field that is passed through the head. The magnetic field creates a small electrical current in the brain but no seizure. Two preliminary studies showed that rTMS led to a statistically significant drop in depressive symptoms without memory loss in severely depressed test subjects. According to an article in *Clinical Psychiatric News* describing the technique, rTMS penetrates the brain without impedance from the scalp and skull, and thus "it is more precise than ECT for stimulating specific areas of the brain."

As of this writing, rTMS research was in its infancy and was being investigated at Columbia University in New York and the Medical University of South Carolina in Charleston. Much more study is needed to determine the treatment's effect on the brain, how it is best administered, and who can benefit from it, Dr. Holly Lisanby, an rTMS investigator at Columbia, told *Clinical Psychiatric News*.

ST. JOHN'S WORT

What is St. John's wort?

St. John's wort *(Hypericum perforatum)* is a yellow, flowering plant that people have been ingesting for an estimated 2,000 years. Over the last fifteen years, St. John's wort ("wort" is Old English for "plant" or "herb") has been used as a remedy for mild to moderate depression in Europe, with few reported side effects. In recent years, St. John's wort has garnered quite a bit of media attention in the United States for both its antidepressant properties and its potential to fight the AIDS virus.

Is St. John's wort effective against depression?

Perhaps. Most of the research was done in Germany. In 1996, the *British Medical Journal* published a meta-analysis of twenty-three scientific studies of St. John's wort involving more than 1,700 outpatients. Overall, the researchers concluded, *Hypericum* extracts were similarly effective as standard antidepressants in the treatment of mild to moderate depression.

Unfortunately, most of the research to date doesn't include enough double-blind, placebo-controlled studies, which characterize the American gold standard when investigating the efficacy and safety of new drugs. That, combined with the lack of uniform preparations of St. John's wort and the lack of sufficient research on drug interactions and long-term side effects, should, at the very least, give you pause if you are considering this remedy. For one thing, there may be other substances in *Hypericum* preparations that have unknown pharmacological properties. Also, St. John's wort may have MAOI-like side effects. In theory, the herb could raise blood pressure if taken with tyramine-rich foods listed in the previous chapter, although this has not been reported in research studies to date.

What are the adverse side effects of St. John's wort?

Digestive problems, allergic reactions, and fatigue have been reported by a small percentage of *Hyper-*

icum users. Sensitivity to sunlight is a more common side effect, so people must use sun protection and avoid other drugs that cause photosensitivity when taking St. John's wort. At the time of this writing, there have been no published reports of serious drug interactions involving St. John's wort, or of toxicity after an overdose of the herb. However, this is no guarantee that St. John's wort is safe. As this herb becomes more prevalently used, it is possible that a different side-effect profile will emerge.

Are American psychiatrists recommending St. John's wort as a depression treatment?

Some are, but the majority are not. Skepticism of St. John's wort centers around these main concerns:

- there is insufficient research into the herb's long-term safety;
- not enough is known about the herb's effectiveness;
- little is known about interactions between St. John's wort and other herbs, drugs, foods, or food additives; and
- there are no standards of purity for the *Hypericum* extracts, tinctures, and teas being sold in American health food stores as food supplements.

Just because a substance is "natural" doesn't always mean it is gentle and harmless. Many powerful drugs used against cancer and other diseases were originally derived from plants. Safety questions and lack of rigorous studies are the main reasons most

American psychiatrists are not recommending St. John's wort, given the alternatives that are known to be safe and effective for depression.

However, that stance could very well change should large-scale studies planned in the United States show the herb to be safe. It is entirely possible that St. John's wort will someday be considered a legitimate weapon in the battle against depressive illnesses. Until then, most psychiatrists think it is too risky or cavalier to use something that is not proven to be safe, even if it appears to be effective.

Skepticism expressed by the established psychiatric community is not stopping many people from using St. John's wort. If you want to give it a try, it would behoove you to first obtain a proper diagnosis if you haven't done so already. There are no data showing the herb can effectively treat major depression, and if this is your diagnosis, taking St. John's wort could be a waste of money and precious time. By delaying standard depression treatment in order to try an unproved remedy, you risk having your illness worsen.

If you have dysthymia, first discuss St. John's wort with a physician, preferably a psychiatrist well versed in state-of-the-art depression treatments. Articles about St. John's wort in the lay press are not 100 percent reliable. If you have dysthymia, maybe psychotherapy is all you need.

What is the proper dosage of St. John's wort?

There are no established guidelines on dosage or length of treatment. However, the daily dosage levels most cited in the medical literature range from 0.4 to 2.7 milligrams of hypericin (*Hypericum*'s presumed active ingredient), or 300 to 1,000 milligrams of

Hypericum extract. Most test subjects seemed to respond in four to eight weeks. You can buy St. John's wort in liquid, capsule, or dried form for tea.

How much does St. John's wort cost?

Random calls to health food stores in the New York metropolitan area revealed that it costs about $8 for sixty 250-milligram capsules, about $11 for one hundred 500-milligram capsules, and about $7 for a one-ounce bottle of extract. Directions on the extract bottle suggest taking ten to thirty drops three times a day, either directly or mixed into tea or juice.

Are any other natural remedies being investigated for use in depression?

A few. Melatonin is an intriguing and popular hormone most commonly used to control jet lag, but it may also have implications in the treatment of depression if taken alone or with antidepressants. But as with St. John's wort, there are no large-scale, randomized, placebo-controlled studies proving melatonin's safety and effectiveness. Those who assume melatonin is benign because it is widely available should consider the case of another hormone, estrogen. Estrogen has been the subject of countless studies, and researchers still aren't sure if it causes breast cancer.

Melatonin is a poorly understood central nervous system hormone produced by the pineal gland and has wide-ranging properties throughout the body. One of those properties seems to be some sort of reciprocal relationship with serotonin, one of the mood-controlling neurotransmitters, which is why melatonin has sparked interest among depression researchers. There is no information on melatonin's long-term safety or side effects. It could turn out to be very good, or it may be very dangerous.

Kava (*Piper methysticum*) is a tranquilizing substance derived from the root of a plant belonging to the pepper family. Kava (also known as "kava kava") is cultivated in Hawaii and the South Pacific and is believed to have been consumed by humans for more than three thousand years. It is used today in Polynesian cultures for spiritual, recreational, and medicinal purposes. Kava reportedly is being investigated by pharmaceutical companies here and abroad.

When ingested (usually in the form of a beverage), kava theoretically may be helpful in agitated depressions and insomnia, but there is no proof. Kava also supposedly has anticonvulsive, diuretic, decongestant, and antiseptic actions, but there are no large-scale, controlled studies demonstrating its safety or effectiveness. Kava may produce hallucinations. And it is potentially addictive since it apparently binds to the same neuron receptors that the powerful anti-anxiety drug, Valium, binds to. Until scientists develop hard evidence of its value and safety in the treatment of depression, kava is best avoided.

Folate (folic acid), an essential vitamin involved in the production of red blood cells in bone marrow, may also play a role in depression. In March 1997, the *American Journal of Psychiatry* published a study showing that people with low levels of folic acid were less likely to respond to antidepressants. Researchers hypothesized that a folic acid deficiency may also play a role in the development of depression.

HYPNOTHERAPY

What is hypnotherapy?

Hypnotherapy is a psychotherapeutic modality that places the patient in a state of relaxed wakefulness and concentration. While in this heightened state of awareness, the patient's mood, memory, or perceptions can change in response to appropriate suggestions by the hypnotherapist. These changes may or may not continue beyond the hypnotherapy session.

Hypnotherapy is typically used for phobias, pain syndromes, insomnia, and anxiety, mainly because the treatment fosters a general state of relaxation. Hypnotherapy is controversial in the treatment of depression. It probably is only slightly helpful for dysthymia, and there is not one shred of evidence that it can do anything for major depression. Hypnotherapy may actually be dangerous if used on extremely paranoid or suicidal patients.

In order for hypnosis to work, the patient must be able to focus his or her attention in a sustained manner. Many severely depressed patients are unable to concentrate long enough to reap any benefit from hypnosis. The whole experience might leave them feeling worse instead of better.

Can hypnotherapy be safely combined with other depression treatments?

Hypnotherapy, if carefully administered by an appropriately trained and experienced psychiatrist or psychologist, may be helpful when used in conjunction with psychotherapy and medication. As with other forms of psychotherapy, hypnotherapy may build patients' sense of self-worth and help them cope with stress in a more positive, creative way.

LIGHT THERAPY

What is light therapy?

Light therapy, also known as phototherapy, is simply exposing yourself to a wide-spectrum artificial light for twenty to thirty minutes a day to relieve symptoms of depression. The light waves used in phototherapy do not include ultraviolet wavelengths, which are carcinogenic.

What types of depression respond to light therapy?

The most common indication for light therapy is major depressive disorder with seasonal pattern, also known as seasonal affective disorder (SAD). People with mild forms of SAD also tend to respond robustly to light therapy. SAD is generally diagnosed when depressive symptoms occur in the late-autumn and winter months and disappear in the spring and summer months.

The causes, diagnosis, and treatments of SAD are addressed more comprehensively in another book in this series, titled *If You Think You Have Seasonal Affective Disorder*.

ACUPUNCTURE

What is acupuncture?

Acupuncture is an ancient form of Chinese medicine in which specific points on the body are stimulated by hair-thin needles that are inserted and twisted, or by an electrical current passed through the needle. The goal is to boost the body's own healing powers by restoring the normal flow of bioelectric energy, or "qi" (pronounced "chee"). Qi flows along bodily pathways known as "meridians," with each set of points corresponding to a particular organ in the body.

Acupuncture is said to affect the structure and function of living tissue without side effects or dependency. Often combined with Chinese herbs, acupuncture is used for a wide variety of physical and mental ailments, including chronic or acute pain, digestive problems, respiratory infections, insomnia, infertility, muscle sprains, smoking cessation, drug addictions, weight control, stress reduction, as well as depression and other mood disorders.

Is there any evidence that acupuncture can effectively treat depression?

Yes. Many practitioners of this five-thousand-year-old technique have reported success in treating patients with depression. In the West, researchers have only recently begun to investigate acupuncture. In one sixteen-week pilot study funded by the U.S. Office of Alternative Medicine, researchers found that acupuncture treatments allayed various symptoms of mild to severe depression. The study, led by John J. B. Allen, Ph.D., an assistant professor of psychology at the University of Arizona–Tucson, randomly divided thirty-eight severely depressed women into three groups: The first group received eight weeks of acupuncture treatments targeted at their depressive symptoms and administered twice a week. The second group received the same amount of general acupuncture treatments that were not meant to treat depressive symptoms. The third group was put on a waiting list for eight weeks before receiving eight weeks of targeted acupuncture. The results of the study: Group one reported a 43 percent reduction in their depressive symptoms, group two experienced a 14 percent reduction in symptoms, and group three reported a 22 percent reduction. Of the women who received targeted acupuncture, more than half were no longer clinically depressed after eight treatments (four weeks). None of the test subjects had been taking antidepressant medication, and none were imminently suicidal, although many had thoughts of suicide.

"We have submitted a grant [application] to conduct a much larger-scale version of our study," Dr. Allen said, "and should those results prove similar, we will then compare acupuncture directly to existing treatments, and we will examine whether acupuncture can prevent relapse." Until more double-blind, controlled studies confirm acupuncture's efficacy, depressed people should consult with a medical specialist before running to the nearest acupuncturist.

Which points on the body were stimulated to alleviate depressive symptoms in Dr. Allen's study?

Points were stimulated in many different regions of the body—the trunk, arms, back, legs, head, and ear.

Were there any side effects to the acupuncture treatments?

None that the researchers could detect. Two of the thirty-eight test subjects dropped out, complaining of discomfort with the needles. Three others dropped out for other reasons, such as moving away or pregnancy.

How can I find a qualified acupuncturist?

Look for someone who is a diplomate of the National Certification Commission for Acupuncture and Oriental Medicine. You can obtain a list of certified acupuncturists by calling the commission at (202) 232-1404. At least thirty-five states regulate acupuncture practice. For information on your state's laws, contact the National Acupuncture Foundation, 1718 M Street/Suite 195, Washington, D.C. 20036, or call (202) 332-5794. This information is also available on the Internet:

> http://www.acupuncture.com/StateLaws/
> StateLaws.htm#26.

Be sure to tell your acupuncturist about any health problems you may have, drugs or medical devices (including cosmetic implants) you are using, and whether you are pregnant.

How much does acupuncture cost?

One national survey revealed the average cost of three months' worth of visits was about $240. Some health insurance plans cover acupuncture. If yours is one of them, get it in writing before beginning treatment, if finances are a concern.

Does acupuncture hurt?

If the practitioner is experienced, acupuncture needles can usually be inserted with minimal discomfort. Acupuncture needles are so thin that ten to fifteen can fit inside a single hypodermic needle.

EXERCISE

How can something as simple as exercise be an effective treatment for depression?

Aerobic exercise, when done routinely, is believed to increase the level of endorphins (the "feel-good" hormones) in the brain. In particular, slow, sustained aerobic exercise, such as swimming, riding a stationary bicycle, or walking, as well as brief, vigorous aerobic exercise, seem to have beneficial effects on all kinds of depression, especially dysthymia. It has been shown that after exercise, levels of serotonin and norepinephrine in the brain increase, which may help alleviate depressive symptoms.

In addition to physiological benefits, exercise offers a psychological boost. Physical activity provides a way of channeling your energy and taking action. This is especially useful if you are bored, withdrawn, or anxious along with being depressed.

Exercise releases tension and can improve your overall sense of well-being. Organized sports, such as volleyball and basketball, require sportsmanship and socialization, which may improve your mood. Given the broad spectrum of exercise benefits, it is no wonder that recreational therapy is often an integral part of hospitalization for depression.

Can exercising regularly prevent recurring episodes of depression?

This area of research has been contradictory. Some studies have shown that exercise does prevent or alleviate depression; others have found that exercise has no impact. More recently, researchers at Johns Hopkins University found that exercising regularly did not prevent depression. This finding was based on annual surveys of almost one thousand, mostly male Caucasian doctors who were followed over a fifteen-year period. The report, part of the Precursors Study, was published by *The American Journal of Public Health* in April 1997.

The findings perplexed and disappointed many

health-care professionals, including the researchers. "I'm one of these people who really advocates exercise and had this belief that physical activity improves mental status," the director of the study, Dr. Lisa Cooper-Patrick, M.D., told *The New York Times* in May 1997. "I was hoping we would show some benefit. But you have to report what you find."

As the *Times* article pointed out, the study's findings may not apply to women and non-whites. And the study did not examine whether exercising during a depressive episode could make symptoms better or worse, or whether exercise offered any measurable psychological benefits.

Despite the controversy, there is no evidence showing that exercise can hurt someone who is in a depressed state. Given the myriad of benefits to a person's physical health, exercise should be a part of virtually everyone's life. If you have been sedentary, be sure to get a checkup before launching into an exercise routine.

Should I try exercising regularly for a period of time before seeking professional help for my depressed mood?

Sure. Exercise is certainly a simple, benign first step, especially if you are only in a funk and do not have a diagnosable depressive disorder. However, symptoms of a significant clinical depression probably won't be relieved by exercise alone. If your mood is still low after exercising every other day for at least two weeks, it is probably time to obtain a professional assessment. That doesn't mean you should stop exercising. Exercise is a good adjunct to any form of depression treatment.

MEDITATION

What is meditation?

Meditation is a stress-reduction technique that brings one's physical, mental, and emotional states into balance. There are several forms of meditation, most of which are steeped in Eastern philosophy but have been popular in the United States for more than thirty years.

One form of meditation can be done sitting or lying down, relaxing your body, and quietly focusing your thoughts on your breath, a word or phrase (mantra), or a mental image. Another form of meditation, known as mindfulness, is "being in the moment" while performing any task—paying close attention, without passing judgment, to all the sights, smells, sounds, and other sensations that you normally overlook or perceive as distracting. Meditation forces you to carve out small blocks of time from your busy day to focus on the present moment and to let go of all other concerns. Any thoughts of the past or future that drift into your consciousness while meditating are allowed to disappear like bubbles in a glass of cola.

By meditating five to twenty minutes once or twice a day, many people feel more relaxed, more alert, and more in control of their feelings. Meditation has been shown to lower blood pressure, reduce heart and respiration rates, and increase alpha brain waves, which are associated with relaxation.

Can meditation alleviate depression?

That depends on how severely depressed you are. Meditation is most commonly used in the West to reduce physical stress, to treat stress-related illnesses and anxiety disorders, and to control pain. It would therefore be helpful in agitated depressions. However, attempts at meditation can backfire on the depressed individual. The reason is that meditation requires concentration. An inability to concentrate is a cornerstone symptom in depression, especially major depression. Failed attempts at meditation threaten to exacerbate an underlying sense of hopelessness and helplessness, which can deepen the person's sense of despair. In general, the more severe your depression, the less useful meditation will probably be.

Depressed people most likely to respond to daily meditation are those with dysthymia and those in recovery from a major depressive episode. Meditation is probably most useful as a preventive strategy. As pointed out in Chapter Three, depressive episodes are often triggered by stressful situations. While meditation cannot stop those situations from happening, it can improve how you respond physically and emotionally to stress.

Unfortunately, any potential benefits of meditation in the treatment of depression are theoretical. If you want to try meditating, realize from the outset that it might not make you feel better. More important, don't get down on yourself if it doesn't work.

Do I need formal training to learn how to meditate properly?

Meditation is easy to learn, and there are many excellent books on the subject. There are also audiotapes with guided meditations. Or, you may choose to take a class in Transcendental Meditation (TM) or another meditation technique. You can learn of TM classes in your area by contacting Maharishi

University of Management, 1000 North 4th Street, Fairfield, Iowa 52557, (515) 472-7000.

Remember, while meditation can be an excellent adjunct, it should not replace medicinal and psycho-therapeutic treatment, especially if you are severely depressed.

Chapter Eight

PREVENTING DEPRESSION

Can depression be prevented?

Not with 100 percent certainty, although there are reasons to be optimistic. According to an ongoing study at the prestigious Western Psychiatric Institute at the University of Pittsburgh Medical School, a recurrence of major depression can be prevented 80 percent of the time if people stay on their antidepressant medication continuously. The subjects involved in the study tend to have major depressions with a presumed strong neurochemical basis.

How to prevent chronic mild to moderate, or "low-grade," depression is less clear. Untreated, an initial bout with dysthymia lasts at least two years in adults and one year in children. If dysthymic symptoms are coming back, your problem may have more to do with your personality style than your brain chemistry. Everyone has an emotional prism through which they view the world. Life can bring losses, disappointments, and joys, and we all react according to our psychology and unique set of experiences. So if, for example, you are a pessimist by nature, working to develop a more optimistic outlook may help you prevent depression in the future.

Timing can also be a factor. If your depressive symptoms always seem to begin when Daylight

Savings Time ends, you may be headed for seasonal affective disorder. Beginning phototherapy as soon as your mood begins to change could help prevent a full-blown case of SAD.

There are also alternative therapies that may help to ward off depressive symptoms or lighten their impact. These therapies will be discussed later in this chapter.

What early warning signs of depression should I look for so I can take preventive measures?

Depression tends to be very insidious, so it is often difficult to become aware that depression is looming, especially if you've never experienced it before. In general, though, be suspicious when symptoms are mild at first, then intensify over time. Also look out for groups of symptoms, not just one.

For example, you might notice an innocuous yet consistent change in your sleep pattern. Perhaps you always went to bed at eleven P.M., fell asleep within twenty minutes and didn't awaken until your alarm clock rang. But lately, you have been tossing and turning up to an hour before falling asleep, and you have begun to wake up earlier and earlier in the morning. In addition, you have a slight change in appetite, an inexplicable crying spell or two, and are feeling distracted and irritable at times. Or you can't muster enthusiasm for activities you normally enjoy, and a sense of sadness, flatness, or dullness seems to be creeping up on you.

Not everyone can tune in to subtle mood alterations. Instead, they notice behavioral changes related to their sinking mood. Difficulty getting out of bed in the morning, being unusually short-tempered with your children, and reading less are some examples. It may take two or more months for all your symptoms to build into a full-blown clinical depression. You'll know when depression hits because the symptoms will be quantitatively greater in strength and in place for at least two consecutive weeks.

Will the same symptoms that signaled my first depression also herald my recurring episodes?

In most cases, a recurrent depression is characterized by similar symptoms that signaled the original depressive episode. So if your first depression involved crying spells, agitation, oversleeping, and severe difficulty in concentration, those generally are the same markers to look for in predicting your next episode.

How and when people perceive early warning signs vary according to personality type. Some people who have had depression before are always looking over their shoulders. If they feel blue one day or didn't sleep one night, they grow concerned—perhaps needlessly—that they're becoming clinically depressed again. Their behavior is not unlike that of many cancer survivors who are supervigilant about monitoring their health status.

At the other extreme are people who are in unconscious denial. They suppress or refuse to acknowledge their symptoms until they are deep into a depressive episode.

Once the episode is over, therapists typically provide patients with a checklist of symptoms that could possibly signal a recurrence. The patients' loved ones and close friends are urged to familiarize themselves with the list so they can guide the patient back into treatment should it become necessary.

If I notice some early warning signs of a recurrence, how long should I wait before contacting my therapist?

Consult your mental health practitioner as soon as you notice some soft, initial signs of depression. Try to do this before those symptoms have been in place for several weeks. It can be very comforting, and even therapeutic, just knowing that someone stands ready to help you.

Can medication prevent full-blown depression if I have clear early warning signs?

The research into treating depression early with antidepressants has produced very mixed results: some data suggest that if you use medication before symptoms become serious, you can prevent a full-blown depressive episode. Other data show that medication doesn't really work until the symptoms are strong and consistent, indicating a full neurochemical change has occurred in the brain.

Given these conflicting data, psychiatrists differ in how they treat early symptoms. Say that you recovered fully from an initial depressive episode years ago but recently developed some mild indications that depression is returning. Some psychiatrists would wait and see if your symptoms can be extinguished with psychotherapy alone. Other psychiatrists would prescribe antidepressants right away. If your psychiatrist recommends medication, recognize that resuming antidepressant therapy is a major commitment. Again, you must wait one to six weeks before the medication begins to work. Then you must remain on medication for a minimum of four months and deal with side effects.

Recent research suggests that going on and off

medication numerous times could make depression more difficult to treat with that particular drug. The cause of this newly recognized phenomenon is not completely understood, but it underscores the concept of remaining on antidepressants for an open-ended period of time after your third depressive episode.

I always get depressed around Christmas and New Year's. Is there anything I can do to prevent this from happening?

Many people's depressions are triggered by holidays or anniversaries of divorce, the death of a loved one, or other sad events. You may prevent these cyclical depressions by anticipating them and doing things to keep your body healthy, your mind occupied, and your stress level at a minimum.

If Christmas is coming up in a month, make sure you are eating properly, if you are not already doing so. That means consuming plenty of fresh fruits, vegetables, whole grains, and fluids; reducing or eliminating your intake of alcohol, caffeine, and sweets; and avoiding all other mood-altering substances. Try to engage in some kind of sport or exercise for thirty minutes at least three times a week. And practice good "sleep hygiene," which means:

- Going to sleep and waking up at roughly the same time seven days a week.
- Avoiding food for two hours before bedtime.
- Avoiding caffeine after noon.
- Avoiding naps.
- Using your bed only for sleeping and making love.

- Going into another room, sitting in a chair, and reading or watching television if you cannot fall asleep within thirty minutes.
- Avoiding vigorous exercise at night.
- Not working right before bedtime.

In addition, try to treat yourself at least once a week: see an uplifting play or movie, go to a comedy club, concert, or ballet; or spend an evening socializing with friends. Whatever you do, don't spend too much time by yourself. And don't be shy about seeking professional help as soon as you feel a depression coming on. It is never too early to talk to a health care provider about your emotional life.

Can reducing stress really block the emergence of another depression?

In many cases, yes. As you may recall from Chapter Three, stress is a common trigger of depression. Cynthia, the freelance writer mentioned in Chapter One, learned this the hard way. Almost a year after recovering from her second major depressive episode, she and her husband invited twenty people over for a dinner party. During the days leading up to the party, Cynthia was shopping, cooking, and looking after her two children by day, and was working late every night in order to meet upcoming deadlines. She was also in touch with a producer who was interested in reading a play that she was almost finished writing.

In retrospect, Cynthia says, the resulting depression was as predictable as it was severe. "One weekend it got so bad that I left my children with my husband and checked into a motel because I thought I was having a breakdown," Cynthia relates. "I just had to get away."

Overloading your schedule when you are prone to depression is tantamount to planning a ski trip when you have a broken leg.

Of course, trying to avoid all sources of stress is unreasonable. You need not live in constant fear that depression may recur. Notice when your moods are low—but do not obsess over them. For some people, depression will happen no matter how hard they try to prevent it, and they shouldn't blame themselves. Perhaps the most reasonable approach is to strive for balance in your life. You are allowed to have a glass of wine, eat a Twinkie, and skip your aerobics class once in a while without putting yourself in depression's path.

If I work on my self-esteem and take other steps to become "mentally healthier," can this prevent depression?

It may. Consider people who are normally filled with a sense of inadequacy, have poor interpersonal relationships, or frequently feel rejected or shunned. When they get clinically depressed, they tend to experience it in a more negative way and wind up feeling even worse about themselves. If, through psychotherapy or support group involvement, they figured out ways to function in a higher, less judgmental manner, they may be able to prevent a recurrence of depression or at least reduce its intensity. This strategy is supported by evidence suggesting that the more mature, emotionally healthy people are, the more likely they are to have a natural buffer against recurrence, particularly of dysthymia and uncomplicated major depressions. Unfortunately, major depression accompanied by melancholic or psychotic features seems to have a life of its own and does not respond as well to efforts at improving overall mental health. The best hope for patients suffering from this form of depression to curb recurring episodes is conventional treatments, such as antidepressants coupled with psychotherapy.

I become extremely depressed every time a relationship with a boyfriend ends. What should I do to prevent these depressions in the future?

If your attachment to an ex-boyfriend was powerful but mature and healthy, it is normal to go through a "mourning period," which can last six to eight weeks after a breakup. If, however, you are overly sensitive to rejection in general, a combination of psychotherapy and antidepressants can probably help you weather your next depression and prevent future bouts.

Some people are very, very dependent on others for their sense of self-worth. They become emotionally attached to their boyfriends much as a child is attached to a parent. When the relationship ends, they feel an enormous sense of abandonment and are unable to function independently. Through psychotherapy, these people can often learn how to develop healthier attachments in the future.

Can any vitamins or foods reduce my risk for depression?

You certainly should maintain a diet that keeps your blood levels of vitamins and minerals within the normal range, but there is no evidence showing that depression can be prevented by taking megadoses of vitamins.

There is evidence that consuming simple carbohy-drates (sugar) and caffeine can bring about a transient increase in mood, which is often followed by a crash.

Can joining a depression support group help prevent future depressive episodes?

Sure. Research has shown that when people spend an inordinate amount of time by themselves, it can adversely affect their mood and their capacity to cope with adversity. The camaraderie fostered through self-help groups probably has an opposite effect.

However, not everyone is comfortable in group encounters. Another tack you might try is cultivating at least one relationship in which you can discuss your depression freely. The mere act of participating in a bowling league or playing basketball once a week may also be protective, because it forces you to be with others on a regular basis.

Can massage therapy or aromatherapy prevent depression?

Anything you do that feels good and cannot hurt you is a positive step. Getting a massage, for example, is an act of self-respect. So is taking a long, luxurious bath to unwind after a difficult day. Being good to yourself on a regular basis raises your self-esteem, and that certainly can have a protective effect against depression.

Can meditation prevent depression?

According to meditation researcher Charles Alexander, Ph.D., of Maharishi University, meditation is a path toward "self-actualization, which is the flip side of depression." When you are self-actualized, Dr. Alexander says, you have resilience, self-worth, and a sense of your mission in life—your personal destiny. All this, he says, gives you a sense of control. Feeling in control is antithetical to feeling powerless, which is very common among depressed people.

Can keeping a journal help me prevent depression?

Writing in a journal can be cathartic, but it probably won't prevent a depression from occurring. It can, however, help you stay in touch with your moods. For example, with each journal entry, you might jot down how you are feeling on a scale from zero to ten. If you notice a string of ones and twos, it might signal the need for professional advice.

Journal keeping may not be a such a good idea for people who tend to obsess over their mood or other aspects of their lives. Basically, you should keep a journal only if it gives you pleasure to write things down. If you choose to keep a journal, don't feel compelled to write in it every day.

What if I take steps on my own to prevent depression but become depressed anyway?

You should be lauded for trying. There is no shame in seeking professional help for a condition that you cannot fully control. Again, diabetes serves as a good analogy. Many diabetics carefully watch their diet and exercise regularly in hopes of reducing or eliminating their need for insulin. When their efforts fail, it isn't their fault. In fact, all their self-help efforts may make medical management of their disease that much easier. The same goes for depressed people.

Self-help strategies can only enhance the effectiveness of medical and psychotherapeutic treatments.

Can children be "inoculated" against depression?

Good parenting and unconditional love can have a preventive effect on depression in children. Good parenting means making children feel lovable and helping them develop self-worth. Children need to know they can express their feelings and still be loved for who they are, not what they do. Good parenting also means teaching children to be autonomous.

If you are suffering from depression, it will be very difficult, if not impossible, to parent effectively. This is one more reason to get proper treatment.

My teenage son talks about killing himself. What should I do?

Take his threats very seriously. If your son is talking about suicide, chances are he has been thinking about it for some time. Threatening suicide is a plea for help, and you must seek it without delay. Many communities have suicide hotlines, which can refer you to a qualified mental health professional and advise you on how to best communicate with your son. If your son won't discuss his feelings with you, encourage him to call the hotline or a person he trusts, be it an adult or peer.

What are the risk factors for suicide?

A previous suicide attempt, a family history of suicide, and articulating a plan are the three most common markers for suicide. Others include being single, white, and female, advancing age, intractable pain, and the death of a spouse or loved one.

Suicidal people also may:

- make statements about hopelessness, helplessness, or worthlessness;
- be preoccupied with death;
- have an unusual amount of guilt or shame;
- have a sense of profound professional or personal failure;
- suddenly feel happier and calmer after a long time of being depressed;
- lose interest in things they once cared about;
- visit or call people they care about;
- get their financial or legal affairs in order;
- give things away;
- be in turmoil over their homosexuality.

When it comes to suicidal thoughts, mental health professionals draw an important distinction between passive and active suicidal ideation. Passive suicidal ideation would include thoughts such as "I wouldn't mind being dead." Passive thoughts are often part of a depressive syndrome and do not usually indicate that suicide is imminent.

Active ideation would include purchasing a gun or stockpiling sleeping pills, and having a plan, such as: "On Sunday, when everyone is at the Little League game, I will kill myself." Even at this stage, however, the vast majority of suicidal people are ambivalent. It is not unusual for them to articulate their plan to a psychiatrist or someone else. This provides an opportunity to help. People who are hell-bent on suicide, however, usually don't tell a soul about their plan and carry it out successfully.

Is it ever normal for people to think about suicide?

Yes. Virtually everybody has considered the notion of suicide, and it is a natural part of the human experience. In the depressed, the thought of suicide often provides a metaphorical door out of a room that has no other doors. In this sense, suicidal thoughts can actually be therapeutic, as long as the person does not act on those thoughts.

How common is suicide among depressed people?

Of the approximately 25,000 people who commit suicide each year in the United States, 70 percent suffer from either depression or alcoholism, studies have shown. Events precipitating suicide among people under age thirty include separation, rejection, unemployment, and legal difficulties. For suicide victims over age thirty, illness is a more prevalent trigger.

I think about suicide every time I'm in a depressive episode. Is there anything I can do to break this pattern before it is too late?

Many people, when they're depressed, experience suicidal feelings. If you did not act upon these feelings in the past, there is no suggestion you will act upon them in the future. If you feel suicidal, it is best to talk it through with someone you trust. The goal should not necessarily be to get rid of your suicidal thoughts. Rather, you should try to identify the causes behind them, since suicide is not always linked to depression. Suicide can be an act of desperation or aggression, or it can be a way of punishing someone. Suicide can also be related to an unconscious fantasy of joining someone who has died.

In many cases, depression-related suicides happen

during the first three depressive episodes—before the person has learned that suicidal thinking is always temporary. On the other hand, many people also become worn out by recurrent depressions and attempt suicide. Ultimately, severe depression and thoughts of suicide go hand in hand. For safety reasons, suicidal thoughts during depression should not be ignored.

Chapter Nine
COPING WITH DEPRESSION

If there are so many effective treatments for depression, why do I need to bother with coping skills?

There are several reasons. It takes up to six weeks for antidepressant medication to block your symptoms. It can take longer should your doctor need to adjust your dose or switch you to a different medication. Likewise, psychotherapy often takes several weeks to make an impact. Anything you can do in the meantime to cope with your disorder on a day-to-day basis will enhance, and perhaps hasten, the effectiveness of your treatment.

Mastering some of the coping strategies outlined below can give you a sense of control, or empowerment, during a time when you feel particularly out of control. These skills can help you preserve relationships at work, home, and in social settings. Finally, learning how to cope with a current depressive episode may enable you to prevent or soften the blow of any future episodes.

What can I do to cope with depression?

Following are tips and strategies that have helped people cope with major depression or dysthymia. Some of the suggested coping mechanisms are self-explanatory. Those that need elaboration are discussed in more detail. The suggestions are not listed in any particular order.

Don't try to employ too many coping skills at once. Pick two or three that seem "doable." If those don't help, try some others. Perhaps just one of the strategies will resonate with you. If that is the case, it may be all you need to make your life more bearable until your depression lifts. At the very least, each of these strategies should provide a healthy counterbalance to the largely negative world in which depressed people dwell.

COPING STRATEGIES

• *Don't skip taking your antidepressant.* If you fail to take your medication as directed, your symptoms may remain the same or worsen.

• *Show up for all your psychotherapy appointments.* It is important to see your therapist as scheduled in order to develop an effective therapeutic relationship and transference (Chapter Five). If you are too ill to leave home, your therapy session can be conducted over the phone.

• *If you feel depressed in the morning, don't fight it.* As explained in Chapter Three, most depressed people feel their absolute worst when they wake up. One way of coping is to give yourself permission to feel horrible in the morning: Cry or wallow in self-loathing, guilt, sadness, and any other negative thoughts and emotions that depression can bring. As you let it all out, realize that your mood will most likely improve as the day wears on. When you are ready, let that realization motivate you to get out of bed, shower, brush your teeth, eat breakfast, and create some structure to your day. Tomorrow morning will bring another opportunity to let your negative emotions flow unabated. As your depression begins to lift, your mornings will become much easier.

• *Try not to spend too much time alone.* Being with sympathetic friends and loved ones may help distract you from your downtrodden mood or give you a shoulder to lean on. Occasional solitude is okay, however, particularly when you feel a need to "fake it" in order to appear happy when you are with others.

• *Whenever possible, avoid people and situations that create stress or make you unhappy.* For Edith, the person to avoid was her mother—a highly critical woman who was a primary trigger for Edith's recurring depressions. During the month Edith was hospitalized for her disorder, she went so far as to tell the reception desk to turn her mother away if she attempted to visit. This move may seem harsh, but for Edith, it was a form of self-protection. "Even now, years later," Edith says, "I see my mother as infrequently as possible."

• *Recognize times of the day when you feel better, and rearrange your schedule to take advantage of those times.* This suggestion is especially relevant in a work environment. For example, don't schedule an important meeting in the morning if this tends to be your worst time of day.

• *Divide large tasks into smaller ones.* You can increase your chances of success by tackling a series of simpler, short-term goals as a way of meeting a more complex, long-term goal. Focusing on one small task at a time also prevents you from feeling overwhelmed. Make sure your long-term goal isn't overly difficult.

• *Set priorities, and stick to them.* It may help to write a "to-do" list and rank each task in order of importance.

• *Lower your expectations of yourself.* You don't expect to do laundry and drive the carpool when you are sick with the flu. Why should you expect yourself to be as playful with your kids or as creative at work when you are suffering from depression?

• *Forgive yourself for not being as productive or friendly as you normally are.*

• *Avoid taking on too much responsibility.* If someone asks you to coordinate your neighborhood block party or become den mother to your son's scout troop, it is okay to say no. You need not share your mental state, just explain that your plate is too full at the moment.

• *Exercise and play sports* (Chapter Seven).

• *Attend sporting, cultural, religious, or social events.* These are sources of great pleasure that may help draw you out of a depressive spiral and put you in touch with like-minded people.

• *Don't make any important life decisions when you are depressed.* Skewed or poor judgment is often a part of a depressive syndrome. If you are depressed while trying to decide whether to quit your job, for example, it will be difficult, if not impossible, to clearly consider all the implications. If you make a major decision while in the throes of any mood disorder, you risk regretting the outcome later.

• *Pray.* Many people believe that prayer can have a healing influence. If you don't want to pray for yourself, pray for someone else who is in need of physical or emotional healing. Or ask someone to pray for you.

• *Listen to or make uplifting music.* Scientific studies have shown that music stimulates the release of the neurotransmitters serotonin and norepinephrine, which can help alleviate depression and create a sense of well-being.

• *Read poetry.* But avoid poems that are too depressing.

• *Hum, sing, or whistle.*

• *Enroll in an adult-education course.* This nurtures intellectual growth and provides an opportunity to be with other people.

• *Volunteer.* Helping others can take your mind off your symptoms.

• *Avoid alcohol and drugs that are not prescribed by your doctor.* Alcohol and illicit drugs can make depressive symptoms worse. Certain legal drugs can cause depression as a side effect or be dangerous if mixed with antidepressants. If you are on an antidepressant, tell your doctor if you are about to take any other prescription or over-the-counter medication (Chapter Six).

• *Remind yourself every day that your feelings of hopelessness are caused by your depressive illness, and that your condition is temporary.*

• *Educate yourself about depression.*

• *Become involved in a self-help group for people with depression or bipolar disorder.*

• *Search the Internet for a chat room for people who are trying to cope with depression.*

• *Read about people who made great accomplishments despite their battles with depression* (Chapter One).

• *Try to maintain decent nutrition even though you may not feel like eating.* This can mean taking a multivitamin every day, or eating more fruit, vegetables, and whole grains when you are hungry.

• *Have one snack a day without feeling guilty.*

• *Cook a special meal and invite someone over to share it.*

• *Rediscover an old hobby or take up a new one.*

• *Put fresh flowers in your home.*

• *Sit in a Jacuzzi, have a massage, or get a manicure.* Anything nice you can do for yourself may improve your mood.

• *Rent funny movies or watch Comedy Central on cable TV.* Laughter triggers the release of endorphins (natural opiates) in the brain.

• *Read "Dilbert" or anything that makes you laugh.*

• *Take a walk or bicycle ride through a park.*

• *Play with children.* Children exude unabashed joy and laughter that can be infectious. Of course, kids can also get on your nerves. Don't feel guilty should this happen. Unless you are the sole caregiver, it's probably best to play with children, or read to them, in short bursts.

• *Buy yourself a gift.* Treat yourself to a pretty dress, a nice piece of jewelry, a new basketball, or your favorite recording artist's latest CD. Even if you don't think you deserve it, the gift can impart a sense of pride and self-worth.

• *Do something nice for someone.*

• *Go to a museum.*

• *Garden.* Gardening is meditative without requiring a tremendous amount of concentration. Digging in the dirt on a beautiful day can help take your mind off your problems and reduce your overall level of stress. Gardening is forgiving; if you don't plant your seedlings exactly six inches apart, they will still grow. Gardening also can give you a sense of accomplishment.

• *Put yourself on "automatic pilot" if you can't get motivated.* Motivation often follows action.

• *If you are invited to a party, put on some makeup or your favorite sport coat and go.*

• *Don't be a perfectionist.* Perfectionism can increase your stress and worsen your depression, especially when you cannot do things perfectly.

• *Spend time with animals.* Research has shown that the simple act of petting a dog or cat can lower blood pressure and reduce stress.

• *Tackle a small home-improvement project.* Installing a shelf, fixing a leaky faucet, or mowing the lawn can instill a sense of accomplishment.

• *Do a "reality check" on your automatic negative thoughts.* For example, if you think, "I'm useless. I can't do anything right," think of the last useful thing you did, such as fixing that leaky faucet, cleaning your kitchen, or teaching your six-year-old niece to tie her shoe.

• *Keep a diary as a means of expressing your thoughts and feelings.* Use it at night to record what you accomplished that day.

• *Don't demean yourself for what you haven't accomplished.*

• *For short-term relief, consider sleep deprivation.* Research has shown that 60 percent of depressed patients on antidepressants enjoy an immediate, dramatic, but temporary reduction in depressive symptoms after staying up for a single night. Forcing yourself to stay up all night is impractical, and even cruel, so mental health professionals don't generally recommend it. Anyway, your symptoms will come back right away if you take a nap the day after staying up all night. Partial sleep deprivation—going to sleep two or three hours early and waking up early—may have a longer-lasting antidepressant effect, especially if practiced two or three times a week. Researchers hypothesize that the lifting of depressive symptoms may have something to do with a reduction in REM-stage sleep.

CAUTION: Sleep deprivation is effective only against major depression; it may have the opposite effect on dysthymia.

How can I help my family cope with my depression?

The first thing you should do is let your loved ones—especially your children—know that they did not cause your depression, and ultimately, they are not responsible for healing it.

Next, you can seek professional help, if you haven't done so already. Bringing a therapist into the picture relieves your family of some of the responsibility and burdens of dealing with your disorder on their own. Therapy also creates a conduit through which healthy change can flow. Encourage your parents, spouse, and children to participate in any family therapy that your therapist might recommend. Family therapy provides insight into your disorder as well as concrete recommendations on how family members can help, given your individual circumstances.

In general, the people you live with should maintain their current roles in the best way they can. In addition, they can let you assume the "sick role"—society's permission for someone to be ill without feeling guilty about it. While you are in the sick role, your family can relieve you of some of your responsibilities until you get better. For instance, if you normally prepare dinner, your spouse and children should take over that task. If your husband is the depressed member of the family and he usually mows the lawn, do it for him or hire a lawn service for a reasonable period of time.

Sometimes, the sick role is taken to unhealthy extremes: family members continue to fawn over a depressed person who has grown excessively dependent. Or the depressed person's inappropriate aggression is tolerated, even when it hurts other members of the family. A therapist can instruct the family on how and when to draw the line, if the family cannot figure it out intuitively. Family therapy is particularly useful when one person's depression serves as a catalyst for family dysfunction. Joining a support group for families of the depressed is another valuable step your loved ones can take.

A FINAL NOTE

Each of the coping mechanisms mentioned in this chapter represents one more reason to be encouraged if you are depressed. As this book has repeatedly emphasized, depression is no longer an intractable disease with unavoidably dire consequences. Depression may cause you to feel helpless and hopeless, but you are neither—and that is the happy irony. Depression is eminently diagnosable and highly treatable with modern, humane therapeutic techniques.

You don't need to suffer. All you need is help.

Glossary

acupuncture: an ancient form of Chinese medicine in which specific points on the body are stimulated by hair-thin needles in order to restore the normal flow of bio-energy

adjustment disorder with depressed mood: tearfulness, sadness, or hopelessness that is triggered by a life change

anaphylactic shock: a potentially fatal allergic reaction

anorexia: a disorder marked by self-starvation

antidepressant: a drug designed to remove depressive symptoms by changing the function of the brain

antihypertensive: any medication designed to lower high blood pressure

arrhythmia: abnormal heart rhythm

atypical depression: form of depression in which there is a sad mood plus some less common symptoms, such as an ability to enjoy pleasurable situations, oversleeping, overeating, and hypersensitivity to criticism

bilateral ECT: electroconvulsive therapy technique using electrodes placed on both sides of the scalp

bipolar disorder: episodes of clinical depression and periods of mania, each of which lasts more than a week; also known as manic depression or manic-depressive illness

bipolar I disorder: a form of manic depression marked by significant manic episodes and quiet depressions

bipolar II disorder: a form of manic depression marked by significant depressions and milder manic periods

bipolar III disorder: an unofficial diagnosis given to someone who is generally depressed but becomes manic when taking antidepressant medication, and who has a family history of depression

brief psychotherapy: any psychotherapeutic modality that focuses on a specific goal and is concluded after several weeks to one year of weekly sessions

classical psychoanalysis: a form of psychotherapy developed by Sigmund Freud that focuses on the patient's childhood, personality development, and unconscious; psychotherapy sessions are usually conducted several times a week for many years

cognitive distortions: inappropriately negative thoughts that may lead to depression

cognitive-behavioral psychotherapy: a form of psychotherapy that helps patients identify negative thinking patterns and change them into positive ones

complete blood count (CBC): a measurement of red and white blood cells; useful in detecting anemia, infections, allergies, and other disorders

convulsion: repetitive overfiring of the neurons in the brain, which leads to various forms of sensory and motor changes; also known as seizure

counseling: a form of talking therapy in which the counselor gives a client hope, guidelines, and information aimed at solving a current problem

cyclothymic disorder: repeated episodes of mild depression and mild manias

depression scale: a psychological questionnaire designed to detect the presence and severity of depression; i.e., Beck Depression Inventory

depression: sadness, pessimism, hopelessness, and related feelings coupled with lack of interest or loss of pleasure lasting a minimum of two weeks

dopamine: one of the brain chemicals believed to play a role in controlling mood

double depression: a condition in which a severe or major depressive episode occurs during a period of dysthymia

dysthymia: a mild, chronic depression or despondency that lasts for at least two years in adults and one year in children and adolescents

dysthymic disorder: see *dysthymia*

electroconvulsive therapy (ECT): a treatment for severe depression that produces a brief, generalized seizure by passing an electrical charge through the brain

electroencephalogram (EEG): a machine that monitors brain wave activity

electrolyte: electrically charged molecules that play a variety of roles in regulating metabolism; electrolytes include sodium, potassium, and calcium

erotic transference: a form of resistance that occurs when a patient falls in love with his or her therapist

first messenger system: a process whereby neurotransmitters hook up with receptors on the outside of brain cells

folate: see *folic acid*

folic acid: an essential vitamin involved in the production of red blood cells in bone marrow and may also play a role in depression; also known as folate

grief: a period of normal sadness and melancholia that occurs after the loss of a loved one

group therapy: a therapeutic setting in which a small group of people exchange information and ideas with the help of a trained facilitator, usually a psychologist, psychiatrist, or social worker

half-life: the amount of time that half of a drug remains active in the body before being metabolized and eliminated

heart block: a condition in which the passage of electrical impulses through the heart's conducting system gets interrupted

heterocyclic antidepressant: an antidepressant with a variable-ringed molecular structure; e.g., Asendin

Hypericum perforatum: see *St. John's wort*

hypersomnia: oversleeping

hypertensive crisis: a sudden, dramatic rise in blood pressure, which may lead to a stroke if not treated; may occur while taking an *MAOI*

hyperthyroidism: an overactive thyroid gland, often caused by an autoimmune disorder resulting in an overproduction of thyroid hormones; symptoms may mimic depression or mania

hypnotherapy: a psychotherapeutic modality that places the patient in a state of relaxed wakefulness and heightened concentration

hypothyroidism: an underactive thyroid gland causing an underproduction of thyroid hormones; symptoms may mimic depression

insomnia: sleep difficulty

interpersonal psychotherapy: a form of psychotherapy that focuses on conflicts, distortions, and difficulties that people have in their relationships with others

kava: a tranquilizing substance derived from the root of a plant belonging to the pepper family; also known as kava kava; may be addictive

light therapy: exposure to bright light in order to relieve symptoms of seasonal affective disorder; also known as phototherapy

Lyme disease: a tick-borne illness that sometimes causes psychiatric symptoms, especially depression

major depressive disorder: a depressed mood or loss of interest or pleasure plus other symptoms that last over a span of two or more consecutive weeks; other symptoms may include significant weight loss, difficulty concentrating, sleep disturbance, fatigue, and feelings of worthlessness

mania: a mood disorder marked by an elevated, expansive, or irritable mood; racing thoughts, feelings of grandiosity, reduced sleep, distractibility, and poor judgment

manic depression: see *bipolar disorder*

meditation: a stress-reduction technique of quietly focusing on the breath, a word, or an action in order to bring the physical, mental, and emotional states into balance

melancholic features: description of a depressed mood that worsens in the morning and fails to brighten, even briefly, when something good happens; may also include feelings of guilt and nervousness or psychomotor retardation

melatonin: a central nervous system hormone secreted by the pineal gland; used most commonly to prevent jet lag, but may also have implications in the treatment of depression

metabolite: a by-product of a drug being broken down by the body

milieu therapy: the ambient therapeutic environment that exists in a psychiatric hospital or unit

mixed mood episode: a diagnosis that is made when symptoms of depression and mania occur simultaneously

monoamine oxidase inhibitors (MAOIs): a class of antidepressants that inhibit an enzyme that breaks down norepinephrine, thus making more of the neurotransmitter available in the brain

mood center: a collection of different neurons spread throughout the brain that control mood

mood disorder: a psychiatric diagnosis that includes depression, dysthymia, bipolar disorder, and mania

mood stabilizer: a drug that blocks both manic and depressive symptoms; i.e., lithium, valproate, or carbamazepine

neuron: brain cell

neurotransmitter: a chemical that facilitates communication between brain cells

norepinephrine: one of the brain chemicals believed to play a role in controlling mood

observing ego: the intellectual part of the psyche that can take a step back and look at life objectively even when emotions are in turmoil

phototherapy: see *light therapy*

physiological stress theory: the notion that when the brain is overloaded physiologically, psychologically, or sociologically, any underlying mental disorder expresses itself; an emotional Achilles' heel

Piper methysticum: see *kava*

placebo effect: a positive or negative effect of a drug that stems from a person's expectations rather than the drug's active ingredient

pluralistic psychotherapy: a form of talking therapy that folds certain aspects of various psychotherapeutic techniques into one treatment

postpartum blues: short period of tearfulness that occurs one to five days after delivery and usually resolves itself without treatment in a few days

postpartum depression: symptoms of major depression that begin within a year of giving birth and last at least two weeks

postural hypotension: dizziness upon standing up abruptly owing to a drop in blood pressure

premenstrual dysphoric disorder: a condition in which a remarkably depressed mood, marked anxiety, and decreased interest in activities regularly occur during the week leading up to menses and remitting within a few days after the onset of menstruation

primary insomnia: difficulty falling asleep

psychiatrist: a medical doctor who specializes in the treatment of psychiatric illness

psychologist: a specialist in the use of psychotherapeutic techniques to treat mental disorders

psychomotor agitation: the visible speeding up of body movements and physical reactions; extreme nervousness

psychomotor retardation: the visible slowing down of body movements and physical reactions

psychopharmacologist: a psychiatrist or other medical doctor who is an expert in medications used to treat psychiatric disorders

psychosomatic illness: any in a range of physical symptoms that can be attributed to a mental, rather than a physical, cause; also known as psychophysiological disorder

psychotherapist: a trained professional who uses psychological methods to help people overcome or cope with mental illness; usually a psychiatrist, psychologist, or clinical social worker; also known as "therapist"

psychotherapy: a talking treatment for mental and emotional disorders using psychological methods

psychotic features: delusions, hallucinations, or other disruptions of perception that accompany depressive symptoms

psychotropic drug: a medication that alters mood or otherwise affects the mind; antidepressants are psychotropic drugs

rapid cycling bipolar disorder: frequent manic or depressive symptoms, which may or may not alternate with each other, in a short space of time

receptor: an area on the surface of a brain cell where chemical messengers (neurotransmitters) attach

recreational therapy: professionally led programs involving sports, dramatics, games, or arts and crafts designed to cultivate interpersonal relationships, socialization skills, and confidence in group settings

REM rebound: a temporary increase in dream intensity and frequency that may occur after halting antidepressant treatment

REM sleep: a dream phase of sleep marked by rapid eye movements

repetitive transcranial magnetic stimulation (rTMS): an experimental depression treatment in which a handheld coil generates a magnetic field that is passed through the head to create a small electrical current in the brain

resistance: a patient's unconscious building of an emotional barrier to the psychotherapeutic process

seasonal affective disorder (SAD): a form of depression caused by changing light cues that occur in late fall and winter; subject of another book in this series: *If You Think You Have Seasonal Affective Disorder*

second messenger system: a cascade of intercellular events that trigger DNA to make changes in brain cells to control mood

secondary insomnia: waking up repeatedly during the night

seizure: see *convulsion*

selective serotonin reuptake inhibitors (SSRIs): a class of antidepressants that increase the availability of serotonin in the brain

serotonin: one of the brain chemicals believed to be involved in controlling mood and states of consciousness

serotonin syndrome: restlessness, tremors, muscle spasms, and confusion that occurs when there is an overload of serotonin in the brain

shock treatment: see *electroconvulsive therapy*

specifier: a term used to fine-tune a broad diagnosis of depression or other mood disorder; i.e., "psychotic features," "melancholic features," or "seasonal pattern"

St. John's wort: a yellow, flowering plant that is being studied in the United States as a treatment for mild to moderate depression

supportive psychotherapy: a form of talking therapy that focuses on the here and now; the therapist provides more guidance, advice, and direction than is available through any other psychotherapeutic modality

tertiary insomnia: waking up earlier than usual in the morning

tetracyclic antidepressant: an antidepressant with a four-ringed molecular structure; e.g., Wellbutrin

therapeutic alliance: the conscious, working relationship that develops between a psychotherapist and patient in order to meet common goals, such as alleviating depressive symptoms

therapist: see *psychotherapist*

traditional psychodynamic psychotherapy: a psychoanalytic modality that looks at the unconscious, early-childhood development, and personality patterns related to a current mental problem

transference: projecting onto a therapist your unconscious thoughts, feelings, and reactions, which were previously experienced with significant others, such as parents or siblings

tricyclic antidepressant (TCA): an antidepressant with a three-ringed molecular structure; e.g., Tofranil

tyramine: an amino acid that can raise blood pressure if a buildup occurs in the body

unilateral ECT: electroconvulsive therapy technique using electrodes on one side of the scalp; usually produces less memory loss than bilateral electroconvulsive therapy

vegetative symptoms: physical signs of depression; e.g., changes in appetite or sleep patterns

vocational therapy: helping patients identify aptitudes and interests and plan their return to work or school

Appendix A: Resources

SUPPORT GROUPS

The support groups listed below were provided by the Self-Help Clearinghouse, Northwest Covenant Medical Center, 25 Pocono Road, Denville, New Jersey 07834-2995. Please enclose a self-addressed, stamped envelope when writing to any of the support groups. Call the groups during business hours only.

National Depressive and Manic Depressive Association
730 North Franklin Street, Suite 501
Chicago, IL 60610
(800) 826-DMDA (3632)
Founded 1986. Provides support and information for patients and families and public education on the biochemical nature of depressive illnesses. Annual conferences, chapter development guidelines, newsletter.

Depressed Anonymous
1013 Wagner Ave.
Louisville, KY 40217
(no phone)
Founded 1985. Twelve-step program to help depressed persons believe and hope they can feel better. Newsletter, phone support, information, referrals, pen pals, workshops, conference, seminars. Information packet ($5), group starting manual ($10.95). Newsletter.

Depression After Delivery
P.O. Box 1282
Morrisville, PA 19067
(800) 944-4773
(215) 295-3994
On-line: http://www.behavenet.com/dadinc

Founded 1985. Provides support and information for women who have suffered from postpartum depression. Telephone support in most states, newsletter, group development guidelines, pen pals, conferences.

Emotion Anonymous
P.O. Box 4245
St. Paul, MN 55104
(612) 647-9712

Founded 1971. Members share experiences, hopes, and strengths using the twelve-step program to gain better emotional health. Correspondence program for those who cannot attend local meetings. Chapter development guidelines available.

National Foundation for Depressive Illness
P.O. Box 2257
New York, NY 10016
(800) 239-1295

An informational service that provides a recorded message of the clear warning signs of depression and manic-depression, and instructs how to get help and further information. For a bibliography and referral list of physicians and support groups in your area, send $5 and a self-addressed, stamped business-size envelope with 98 cents postage.

Mood Disorders Support Group, Inc.
P.O. Box 1747
Madison Square Station
New York, NY 10159
(212) 533-MDSG

Founded 1981. Provides support and education for people with manic depression or depression and their families

and friends. Guest lectures, newsletter, rap groups,
assistance in starting groups.

National Organization for Seasonal Affective Disorder
(NOSAD)
P.O. Box 40190
Washington, DC 20016
(no phone)
Founded 1988. Provides information and education on the
causes, nature, and treatment of seasonal affective
disorder. Encourages development of services to
patients and families, research into causes, and treatment.
Newsletter.

SELECTED DEPRESSION WEB SITES

http://www.psycom.net/depression.central

http://members.aol.com/depress/children.htm

http://www.schizophrenia.com/ami/diagnosis/depress.html

Bipolar Disorder Web Sites

http://www.schizophrenia.com/ami/diagnosis/manicDep.html

http://www.frii.com/~parrot/bip.html

PROFESSIONAL ORGANIZATIONS

American Psychiatric Association
1400 K Street, N.W.
Washington, DC 20005
phone: (202) 682-6325
fax: (202) 682-6255

American Psychological Association
750 First St., N.E.
Washington, DC 20002-4242
(202) 336-5500

American Society of Clinical Psychopharmacology
P.O. 2257
New York, NY 10116
(212) 268-4260

OTHER INFORMATION SOURCES

Depression Awareness Recognition and Treatment (D/ART)
5600 Fishers Lane
Rockville, MD 20857
For free brochures on depression and its treatment, call:
(800) 421-4211
On-line: http://www.nimh.nih.gov/newdart/gen_fact.htm
*National public and professional education program
sponsored by the National Institute of Mental Health.
D/ART's goal is the alleviation of suffering for the
1 in 10 American adults with depressive illness, and is
based on more than fifty years of medical and scientific
research on depression.*

National Alliance for the Mentally Ill
200 North Glede Road, Suite 1015
Arlington, VA 22203-3754
(703) 524-7600

National Institute of Mental Health
Division of Communications
5600 Fishers Lane
Rockville, MD 20857
(301) 443-4536

National Mental Health Association
1021 Prince Street
Alexandria, VA 22314-2971
(703) 684-7722

Appendix B:
Further Reading

DEPRESSION

Prozac and the New Antidepressants, by William S. Appleton (Plume, 1997).

The Beast: A Reckoning with Depression, by Tracy Thompson (Putnam and Sons, 1995).

Listening to Prozac, by Peter B. Kramer (Penguin, 1994).

On the Edge of Darkness: Conversations about Conquering Depression, by Kathy Cronkite (Doubleday, 1994).

Prozac Nation: Young and Depressed in America, by Elizabeth Wurtzel (Houghton Mifflin Company, 1994).

How to Heal Depression, by Harold H. Bloomfield, M.D. and Peter McWilliams (Prelude Press, 1994).

Undercurrents, by Marth Manning (HarperSanFrancisco, 1994).

Depression: The Mood Disease, by Francis Mark Mondimore (Johns Hopkins University Press, 1993).

You Are Not Alone, by Julia Thorne with Larry Rothstein (HarperCollins, 1993).

Understanding Depression, by Donald Klein, M.D., and Paul Wender, M.D.—founders of the National Association for Depressive Illness (Oxford, 1993).

The Depression Handbook, by Mary Ellen Copeland, (New Haringer Publications, 1992).

Overcoming Depression, by Demitri F. and Janice Papolos (Harper-Perennial, 1992).

From Sad to Glad, by Nathan S. Kline, M.D. (Ballantine Books, 1991).

Feeling Good: The New Mood Therapy, by David Burns, M.D. (Signet, 1980).

BIPOLAR DISORDER

An Unquiet Mind: A Memoir of Moods and Madness, by Kay Redfield Jamison (Alfred A. Knopf, 1995).
A Brilliant Madness: Living With Manic-Depressive Illness, by Patty Duke and Gloria Hochman (Bantam Books, 1992).

Index